'We have lived through ⸻ ... ⸻ has been banished from the ⸻ ... ⸻ ave peddled different philosop⸻ ... we begin a new century we have come back to the indisputable truth that faith works. Faith transforms individuals as well as communities. That is why I wholeheartedly endorse Faithworks.'

Richard Chartres, Bishop of London

'In co-operation with national and local government and the private sector, faith communities and the voluntary sector have an important and distinctive role to play in the provision of social welfare in this country. . . The faith-inspired work of Christians can contribute in no small measure to promoting the common good of our society. . .'

Cormac Murphy O'Connor, Archbishop of Westminster

'It is impossible for our faith to be real if it is not put to work on behalf of the poor, disadvantaged and those who are the fringe of society. Politicians and statutory organisations need to recognise and appreciate that churches could be invaluable partners as they possess the largest volunteer force in every community and are experienced and efficient providers of many essential services.'

Mark Sturge, General Director,
The African and Caribbean Evangelical Alliance

This book is dedicated to Beatrix Grace
in the hope that she will continue to delight those around her
with God's love and joy
and so bring Christ's transforming life into the world.

FAITHWORKS 2:
Stories of Hope

STEVE CHALKE
WITH
TOM JACKSON

KINGSWAY PUBLICATIONS
EASTBOURNE

ISBN 1 84291 014 0

Published by
KINGSWAY COMMUNICATIONS LTD
Lottbridge Drove, Eastbourne, BN23 6NT, England.
Email: books@kingsway.co.uk

Book design and production for the publishers by
Bookprint Creative Services, P.O. Box 827, BN21 3YJ, England.
Printed in Great Britain.

Contents

Acknowledgements

We are immensely grateful to all those who have given us so much help in completing this project. It would never have happened without the hours of generous assistance poured in by Sarah Jackson, Libby Ferguson and Doug and Angela Bacon. We are indebted to those who graciously gave up valuable time to tell us their stories, and to their colleagues who (often unmentioned) work behind the scenes with them.

Our many thanks are also due to Simon Downham, Aredi Pitsiaeli, Nathan Oley, Tina Millen, Kate Fletcher, Mannie Stewart, Penny Relph, Sandy Millar, Dave Roberts, Jess Hunter, to all at Oasis, St Paul's Hammersmith and Kingsway, and to our families and friends for the unstinting support that they have given us.

Foreword

Bishop Lesslie Newbigin once wrote:

> Christian programmes for justice and compassion severed
> from their proper roots in the liturgical and sacramental life of
> the congregation lose their character as signs of the presence
> of Christ, and risk becoming mere crusades, fuelled by a
> moralism that can become self-righteous; and the life of the
> worshipping congregation severed from its expression in com-
> passionate service in the secular community around it risks
> becoming a self-centred existence, serving only the needs and
> desires of its members.

I cannot remember a time when it was so urgent for the
church of Jesus Christ in all its rich variety to pull together
to demonstrate the love of God in the practical work of
compassion and service, and I am convinced that the
recent outpouring of God's Spirit has inspired many new
initiatives and individuals in renewed acts of kindness and
self-sacrifice. It is extremely encouraging, though we have
a long way to go!

The stories told in this book are a wonderful inspiration to us all, and speak of the practical hope that the church brings when it is faithful to the call of God. They are an encouragement to us to go and do likewise.

I believe that the Faithworks initiative is a timely and important one for the church across the UK. Let us all seize the opportunities now to begin to recover our communities for Christ.

The Reverend Prebendary Sandy Millar
Vicar of Holy Trinity Brompton

Introduction

The church has an indispensable role to play in building communities and providing welfare up and down our land. That's the simple yet profound message of the *Faithworks* movement. Because churches are locally based and able to adapt imaginatively to the issues that surround them, their capacity to transform local neighbourhoods is unrivalled. No one is better placed to deliver the vital practical and spiritual hope which every individual and community needs in order to thrive. *Faithworks* is an idea whose moment has come.

Stories of Hope is the second book from *Faithworks*. It tells eight stories from churches of different denominations across the UK who are effectively tackling a wide range of social issues. From debt advice to counselling for domestic violence, from after-school projects to sports clubs, from education to youth work and from arts initiatives to vocational training – each chapter tells an inspiring story of a local church or individual that has responded to a God-given sense of purpose and direction.

11

Told in the words of the people concerned, the stories are open and revealing accounts of the struggles and joys, challenges and opportunities, frustrations and breakthroughs of a faith that has changed a community. There is much we can learn from them. The imaginative solutions brought to the different needs they face, the way in which common themes start to emerge and the examples of working in partnership with local government and other agencies all help to point the way for those of us with a desire to bring new hope to our local communities.

The organisations listed at the end of each chapter have not necessarily been involved with the specific projects concerned, but they can offer advice to groups who wish to develop similar initiatives. For general advice on developing community involvement, see the 'Useful Contacts' list at the back of the book.

We hope that these stories will inspire you to see how your faith can make a difference in *your* community.

Steve Chalke and Tom Jackson

1. The Thornbury Centre, Bradford

Paul Hackwood was appointed as the Chair of the Thornbury Centre in June 1997. The centre, which has been set up by the church of which Paul is vicar, and is run in association with a range of other organisations in the area, plays a unique role in restoring and rebuilding relationships in what has become a very divided urban community. It hosts a wide number of projects, including an arts initiative, work with the elderly, training programmes and Homestart, which is part of a national initiative to support family life. Now aged 40, Paul is married to Josie. They have two children aged six and three.

Thornbury is a suburb one-and-a-half miles to the east of Bradford city centre. It is the second most disadvantaged ward in Yorkshire and suffers from high levels of poverty and crime. The community, which is very multi-cultural, has seen a steadily increasing amount of racial tension and violence in recent months.

Crime has become so endemic here that most people are largely unable to confront it. It has become almost impossible for those who would like to make a stand against it to do so in practice. The police are wary of getting involved in situations where they may be accused of being biased in favour of one racial community over another. They find themselves working against huge odds with few resources. It has become very difficult for them to effectively police the area at all. Our community has become a place where people have to live fairly heroic lives if they are to do the best for themselves and their families.

Thornbury has the second highest rate of drug arrests in Bradford (which is itself one of the worst areas for drug use in the country). The drug problem is, in turn, a big factor in the high level of HIV and AIDS in the area. Another problem is the escalation of vandalism and property crime. Within the first month that our community centre opened we had suffered £15,000 worth of theft and damage. There is also a lot of intimidation and violence. For instance, our church youth group had to be closed down after a member of our staff was stabbed there.

The decay in the community is so great that it has become accepted as the norm. For example, those who do not take drugs are often considered abnormal. I work with one young lad in his early twenties who decided twelve months ago to give up drugs and go to a rehabilitation clinic. Having returned clean, he is now quite often stopped on the street and beaten up if he refuses to buy drugs from the dealers. So the whole context of the community works against him breaking free.

My office overlooks a primary school playground. A few weeks ago I looked out of my window to see two young lads selling drugs outside the school gates. People would walk up to them and hand over some money and be given a little package of white powder in return. It was particularly shocking to see this happen so flagrantly outside a school. So I went over and asked them to move. When they refused, I decided to stay with them and point out that they wouldn't be able to sell many drugs with a vicar standing next to them! They responded by calling their mates on their mobile phones, and the next thing I knew I was surrounded by 30 or 40 muscular lads jostling around and trying to intimidate me.

I was feeling quite fearful for my safety. However, I didn't feel I could back down, and so I said, 'No matter what you do, I am not going to move from here until you leave.' They became increasingly aggressive and got right to the point of physically assaulting me. However, just at that moment, a local Muslim leader drove past and stopped to see what was going on. When I explained what I was doing, he decided to stand with me. He told the youths (some of whom were also Muslims) that he too would not leave until they went. Eventually, they gave up and, after spitting on us both, moved on.

This story is typical of the kind of intimidation and lack of respect for the law that is commonplace here. Working in Thornbury raises huge questions about how the Christian faith works in this kind of context. How does our understanding of God relate to an inner-city community that is fragmented, lawless and where nothing seems to go right? As I've thought this through, I have come to believe that because God is at work in the world, if the church is not engaged at the centre of the neighbourhood, then it is failing to participate in his mission. I have become convinced that unless we make the choice to step out of old models of being the church into new ones, then our congregations will continue to dwindle and die.

I feel that in a very real sense God has been preparing me for my role here in Thornbury over many years. I grew up in the Midlands near Birmingham, and started going to church at the age of 13. I trained as a social worker before being ordained. Over the years my experience of church has been very broad, and I have worked and worshipped in all sorts of environments from Anglo-Catholic congregations through to charismatic evangelical ones. In my last job I was a social responsibility officer in St Albans, and when I was appointed to St Margaret's in Thornbury in June 1997, I knew I had the opportunity to try and implement the sort of project that I had been able to help others set up down there.

The site of the Thornbury Centre has been home to St Margaret's Church since the beginning of the twentieth century. A traditional stone building was the base for the worshipping community until the late 1980s, when cracks started to appear in the chancel. Within a week a Dangerous Buildings Notice was served on the PCC, and as a result the whole building had to be demolished. This forced the congregation to move into an adjacent hall, and over the next few months to think carefully about the way ahead. Gradually, they came to the recognition that their church consisted of the people rather than the stone building. This was a very significant insight because it enabled them to see the value of their role as Christian people in the neighbourhood. Because of this, they decided that they didn't want just to build another church building, but

rather to build a centre that would serve the wider community. It was out of this vision that the Thornbury Centre
was born.

The church started to attract funding from a variety of
different sources. The commitment of the congregation is
shown by the fact that, although they were a group of less
than 50 people, they managed to raise £250,000 between
them. This was at the cost of much personal sacrifice. For
example, I know pensioners on state pensions here who
have tithed consistently for ten years. They also managed
to raise funding of a further £2.5 million through bodies
such as the Millennium Commission, the European Union
and the local Regeneration Development Agency.

It was at this stage that the existing vicar left and the
Bishop of Bradford started looking for someone else who
could develop the work. I was appointed on the basis of
my previous experience, and I am now the vicar of the
parish, as well as the chair of the centre. Since there was no
building, my induction took place on the grassy site where
the centre was to be built. Instead of a set of keys to the
church, I was given the plans for the building! One of my
first jobs was to work with other members of the church to
raise another £500,000 of funding, and then to turn the congregation's attention to getting the new building built and
to setting in place the organisation and structure to run it.

Having started the building work in February 1998, it
was finally completed in April of the following year, and
officially opened by Princess Alexandria twelve months
later. We asked the architect to design the centre in a way
that made us open to the community as a church, but also
gave us some private space which we could use together

as a congregation. As a result, we have a very distinctive
building. The architect has created an extremely light and
airy building with a central atrium, which links all the
rooms in the building. When you want to pass from one
room to another you always have to walk through the central communal area. What that does is create connections
and means that the ethos of our building is the same as
that of our overall work – we are here to create connections
between people.

As you enter the building, you are greeted by a cafeteria
area. We wanted to have a space that welcomed people,
and food is very welcoming. On the left is the worship
area, which is entered through a stained glass door so as to
give the impression of something special lying behind it.
At the back of the building is a community hall and bar
which gets used for local celebrations. As well as that we
have seven meeting rooms of varying sizes. Some of these
are used by the projects that work from the building, and
others are let out to other local organisations and businesses
in order to create some revenue with which to run the centre.

The Thornbury Centre's overarching goal is to tackle the
underlying problems that threaten the community. I
believe that the core issues are far deeper than the lawless
escalation of drugs, vandalism and violence. These problems are symptomatic of a greater underlying sense of
hopelessness, which is caused by the lack of options for
local residents, particularly for young people. When there
are few jobs or prospects, and unemployment runs at
25 per cent, how can you imagine a future of brighter
possibilities? It's an environment that is corrosive and

dehumanising. Without hope, people cannot grasp the importance of having a system of values which will benefit anyone, or anything, beyond themselves. As a result, they tend to do things that centre on their own survival rather than working to develop community and relationships with their neighbours. And worst of all, it's a vicious circle because the resulting social fragmentation only reinforces the overwhelming sense of hopelessness.

A big part of what we are trying to do is to give people the opportunity to be hopeful about the future. I believe that it is a very important part of our Christian message to say that human beings are creatures of hope. As Christians, we believe that God is in the process of enhancing our humanity and making us the best we can possibly be. We believe that every human being is full of potential. We believe that God is slowly establishing a future that is positive. The Bible calls us to a vision of community where all live under God's authority and recognise the humanity and worth of others; a community where all people live together in an atmosphere of peace, justice and truth. Without this vision of tomorrow there is no point in having any values because they have no ultimate goal to take us to.

We believe that the best way of empowering the local residents of Thornbury is to give them the opportunity to address their needs in their own way. As a matter of principle, we will not run a project unless it has been asked for by the community. A lot of our work continues to be based on the original audit that we did about four years ago in order to find out what people wanted in the building. However, we also regularly carry out door-to-door surveys, because we want to keep listening to local people, and let them know that they have a voice.

We try wherever possible to ensure that any service that is provided in the centre is run by and shaped by local people. We work hard to give people a say in the management of the projects, and to ensure that they feel a real sense of ownership of them. We have set ourselves against creating any sort of relationship of dependency. It's not that we don't steer things and guide them; it's just that we don't steer and guide them in directions people don't want to go!

It has been difficult to find clear models for the kind of work that we as a church are engaged in. Models that focus solely on the congregation won't work for us, because they end up separating us off from the community. But, equally, models which are too heavily community orientated would end up destroying the congregation because the needs in the area are endless.

So, our response has been to pray and look for the activity that God is already engaged in within Thornbury, and try to join in. For instance, one area where we feel God is at work is in restoring relationships and unity within the community. So one of the things we are focusing on is building our relationship with other faith communities. We do not in any sense abandon our Christian perspective. However, we do recognise that because relationships across the ethnic communities are so bad, they have a dehumanising influence on the whole of the neighbourhood. People are so alienated that, for example, the Muslims won't have any contact with the Hindus and Sikhs, while many white British young people won't even walk down streets where the Muslims live, and vice versa.

We have tried to address these issues by working hard with the other religious communities. We have seen great progress and I believe that God's Spirit is at work creating a new sense of community in Thornbury. We have been fortunate to have a really good South Indian pastor, called Solomon Joseph, working with another church in the area, who has been a guiding force behind much of this progress.

It has been important for us to create the right governing structures. But because the church and the wider community use the same resource, perhaps there will always be a bit of tension here. On one hand, we don't want to see the church dictate to the community, so we have tried to frame our constitution as carefully as possible. We have set up a charity that is made up of seven representatives from the church council, two from the local authority, three from the local community, four who represent the users of the centre and one from the local school. What that means is that the church has a major say in what goes on (some of the user group representatives are also associated with the church), though legally we only have a third of the votes. Therefore we have to listen actively to what other people have to say, which I think is a good discipline because churches have often been guilty of setting their own agenda without really engaging with their communities. But we also have some level of protection because the constitution prohibits certain activities that would be inappropriate or against our values. For example, the worship of other communities is not allowed in the building and the incumbent has a say in whether or not any particular activity is conducive to the central ethos of building up the community.

Since the constitution cannot be changed without two-thirds of the votes there is a level of protection there, though we always try to work as openly with the community as possible.

We run a wide range of projects out of the centre. Some have been initiated by the church, while others are run by or in association with other organisations. They are all non-profit making as required by the constitution, and whatever surplus they make gets ploughed back into the overall work of the centre. We are constantly on the hunt for new ideas. One person on our board also sits on the Local Regeneration Board Partnership, and if they identify any good project ideas that need a base to develop from, then we look to see whether or not they correspond with the kinds of need that local people have identified and whether they fit with our ethos. If there is a significant match then we will positively consider working with them.

One of the projects that we run out of the centre is called Artswork. It grew from the idea I had when I first arrived that there was a lot we could do to help local people foster their creativity. As we looked at the possibilities, we came across a woman by the name of Bev Morton who had a very similar vision. As a result, we set the project up together. The aim is to help put local people who have creative ideas for regenerating the community into contact with professional artists in order to help them achieve their goal. Artswork has proved very successful, and over the last two years we have involved about 7,000 people in the initiative. In fact, it has grown so much that we have recently registered it as an independent charity. We have implemented a variety of ideas – from commissioning public art and sculptures for some of the local housing estates, right through to producing a local authority calendar each year, which incorporates paintings and collages from both children and adults and is distributed to every house in the neighbourhood. Some of the paintings from the calendar have even been blown up and posted on roadside advertising hoardings right across the city. It is great when a local person who has never been given much opportunity to express their creativity sees their artwork as they ride somewhere on a bus or in a car. As you can imagine, it gives them a tremendous buzz of pride and affirmation. Another thing Artswork does every year is to create puppets and costumes for the Bradford carnival – last year we had nine floats full of people dressed up from the local estates in the procession!

We have developed our work with older people in partnership with the local council. Our community faces a considerable problem in relation to elderly people suffering from a sense of isolation, intimidation and fear. Because of the level of crime in the area, it is almost impossible to get them to come out after dark, and in winter they can feel forced into staying in their homes for days on end. Our senior citizens' work is centred around Wednesdays. We start with a service at ten o'clock in the morning, which about 30 people come to, and afterwards have a luncheon club, which about 65 people now attend. The project has really taken off under its own steam and we don't have to do anything except provide the food. Many people then stay on for most of the afternoon. We have a local police officer who regularly pops in to chat about crime preven- tion issues. We also invite other speakers along – for instance recently someone from the council came in to talk about benefits advice. We are presently looking at the possibility of setting up other leisure activities around the afternoon group. Once a month we also host a tea club, which runs a programme that includes invited speakers and feature films. The organising group also plans other community activities for their age group, such as day trips, etc. We are now actively looking at how we expand this work.

The library is run by the local authority and hosted by us at the centre. We originally set it up as a neighbourhood information centre to facilitate communication between organisations like the council or the local health service and the residents. Our job was to act as the disseminator of lots of informative brochures and leaflets. But now as a joint initiative, it has grown into a fully-fledged library staffed by a local authority librarian, assisted by a community resident. The idea behind this aspect of the scheme is to both build a bit more community into the library as well as provide a local person with some excellent training for the job market.

We place a big emphasis on training in the centre. For instance, Bradford College uses our facilities to teach a course in mature studies which enables people with no educational qualifications to gain a foundation certificate within 18 months, which will then qualify them for university entrance. They also run a very popular Learning English as a Second Language course. On top of that, we have an IT training suite that is run in partnership with the council. It comprises 24 computers, which are used to help local people upgrade their computer skills and gain qualifications. We run weekly courses in desk-top publishing, word processing, spreadsheets and databases. We also run regular courses in various other skills, including such things as dressmaking and line dancing.

We run Homestart as part of a national initiative that uses volunteers to work alongside families who need support. For example, a parent who is struggling to cope with a child who is ill or who has behavioural problems, or a mum or dad that just needs a bit of a break. Our volunteers are all fully trained in child care and support, including child protection, and will commit to spending a morning or afternoon a week in each home, working with the parent and acting as a carer. To supplement Homestart, we also run a nursery and child care project called 'Child Works' and have a youth project, which is supervised by the local authority.

Our café is open every day and has three aims. First of all it tries to create a heart for the centre. We try to provide a safe space where older and younger people can come and eat together in a public but non-threatening environment. For instance, one woman who comes was severely agoraphobic until the café opened, but now she feels comfortable enough to come in every day. Second, the café also enables us to train people in catering skills. We have had many local people who have qualified in food hygiene to NVQ level 2 and then gone on to find a permanent job. Third, although the café itself runs at a loss, the catering service generates income, because we do outside bookings for local businesses and community organisations, as well as internal work for training and conference events held in our building.

We also have a bar adjacent to the main hall. It is run by the church congregation and is used largely for community events. Once again, any profit it makes gets ploughed back into other church activities. The congregation also organises bingo in the hall as a community outreach and runs the Emmaus evangelism course for people who want to know more about the Christian faith. We find this course always includes a number of people who have arrived there via our other activities.

We have 15 full-time staff and a much larger number of volunteers. Around 25 members of the congregation volunteer to work specifically for the centre. We treat all volunteers just as if they are employees. So although they don't get contracts of employment, they do receive job descriptions, supervision and appraisals, and are part of staff meetings.

We have worked hard to develop good relationships with other agencies that are engaged in delivering welfare in the community. Many of them have used our facilities and seem to like the physical attractiveness of the building and the fact that we create a space where they can come and work without any interference.

Our relationship with council officers is very good, and they have been supportive of us from the beginning. We have also developed good links with the Regional Development Agency. However, we have sometimes had a mixed response from some local community leaders, who have been very suspicious of us. When we have been attacked, the key has been not to fight back, but neither to compromise our objectives. We feel it is important to try and build good relationships by not looking for trouble, but at the same time to refuse to be intimidated by them.

We never use government money for evangelism, not only because the conditions of such funds specifically exclude this, but also because we would be uncomfortable with it anyway. We now have a turnover of half-a-million pounds per annum, but have worked hard at not becoming so dependent upon grants that our prophetic edge is undermined. We have, therefore, tried to create a one-third/two-thirds split, where though one-third of our total income comes through grants such as the lottery, the other two-thirds is self-sustained and made up from letting our facilities for conferences, as well as proceeds from the bar, the café and so on.

We believe it is morally wrong to make the use of any service dependent upon a faith allegiance. However, if we are asked, or if it is otherwise appropriate, we will always openly and honestly talk about what we believe. We never put a wrapper on our faith, which includes our dealings with the other faith communities, but neither do we push it insensitively.

If someone were to say that our work in the community is a distraction from our duty to evangelise, then I would say that they don't understand what evangelism is. Evangelism is about telling people the good news of Jesus Christ in a way that affects them both personally and socially. But it's a message that needs to be communicated through the things we do, as well as verbally. In our society as a whole, and certainly in Thornbury, there are too many spoken words. It is only when people see that those words are backed up with integrity that they are really heard. I believe it is no coincidence that our congregation numbers have almost doubled since we opened the centre.

What we are really trying to do is to create an alternative. I don't think we can ever change the whole world, or even, for that matter, the whole of Thornbury. But we can create an alternative that says there is a different way to live and relate to others. You don't have to live solely for your own survival; it's possible to live in a way where you trust others and are prepared to listen and work together with them. Of course, all this is a journey. If we could have seen ten years ago what we are doing now, we would have been too afraid to begin. All we did back then was to take the one small step we could, and then another, and another – until we have reached the point where we are today. And that first step was simply trying to catch a vision for what was possible.

None of what we have done has been easy. In fact, it has been absolute agony. I have been repeatedly tested beyond my own strength and training, and sometimes it has challenged the very depth of my faith. One problem is the level of conflict that you get whenever you try to start something new. People can get very suspicious. They go to all sorts of lengths to check that you know what you're doing, and that you're able to deliver what you said you would deliver. I have experienced some personal attacks that have left me absolutely devastated. Once I went through weeks when I hardly slept because I was so anxious about it all. In fact, I have lived through four years of self-doubt in a way that I would never have imagined was possible before.

To be truthful, I feel I have been challenged at a personal level as well as enriched by the Thornbury experience.

And yet I know God has kept me going when I've most needed it. I can honestly say that without the empowering activity of God's Spirit, Thornbury would never have happened. There have been times when I've reached the point where I couldn't go on any further, and then I've felt a little nudge to keep me going as new possibilities have opened up.

As for my joys, it is a wonderful privilege to participate in what God is doing. And to that end, one of my greatest moments was last year when a local group of Muslim leaders said 'the Church of England is good news for this community'. Even if I don't carry anything else away from this place other than that, then it has been worthwhile.

Relevant contacts

Age Concern
Astral House
1268 London Road
London SW16 4ER
Tel: 020 8679 8000
Email: infodep@ace.org.uk
www.ace.org.uk

Churches Community Work Alliance initiates, supports and encourages community work in the life of churches.
CCWA
24 Tynesdale Close
Wylam
Newcastle upon Tyne NE41 8EX
www.ccwa.org.uk

Home Start provides practical support to young families under stress in their homes.
Brian Waller
2 Salisbury Road
Leicester LE1 7QR
Tel: 0116 233 9955.
Email: info@homestart.org.uk
www.Home_Start.org.uk

The Shaftesbury Society produces a guide to community research and has developed the 'Action for Change' network which offers support, training and materials for church-based social action.
Church Development Services
16 Kingston Road
London SW19 1JZ
Tel: 020 8239 5555
Email: info@shaftesburysoc.org.uk
www.shaftesburysoc.org.uk

2. The Community Debt Advice Centre, Burgess Hill

Heather Keates' own experience persuaded her that debt is one of the most significant and yet least emphasised problems to face our society. By way of a response, in 1997 she established a Community Debt Advice Centre that runs through her local church in West Sussex. To date she has helped over 500 people find a pathway out of their debt, and since 1999 has helped 18 similar centres all over the country to get started. Heather is married to Tim and they have four children.

I discovered the trauma of debt through my own experience. I grew up in a very comfortable middle-class family and never really went without. After school I started training as a teacher before marrying Tim. Everything was going well. I had a good sense for managing our finances, because my parents had taught me to take responsibility for my own actions. From a young age I was taught that if I didn't make my pocket money last it was my problem. I did not really understand the difficulties that other people faced and I thought that if someone was in debt it was

their own fault. I just didn't realise how many people are
never taught, either at home or at school, what a budget is
or how to look after their finances.

Then, through circumstances beyond our control, Tim
and I got into debt. It started in 1989 when our first child
was born and my husband lost his job in a graphic design
studio. He decided to set up his own business, but it was
more costly than we had reckoned on and we didn't have
the means we needed behind us. I was looking after our
newborn child and was unable to help. Gradually, our
financial situation deteriorated. Then, our third child was
born two-and-a-half years later with a major heart defect
and between us we had to spend four months in hospital
about 45 miles away. As a result, we accumulated the costs
of child minders and travel to and from the hospital. Tim
was having to look after the house and the family, and was
unable to run the business properly. Six months later we
went on a much-needed holiday to France, and there the
baby was taken ill and eventually died. Although we had
insurance, there was a whole series of associated costs of
repatriation that we had to cover. In September 1992, we
returned to England devastated, and at that time the business failed and our house sale fell through. Everything was
in tatters. We did not know what to do. We dreaded the
phone ringing in case it was someone asking for payment
of a debt. We had to go and explain ourselves to the
bank, but no one there seemed to want to know what
we were going through. We felt incredibly isolated and
unsupported. It took a very long and painful time for us to
get back on our feet again. Eight-and-a-half years later
we are still paying the debt and we will probably still

be paying it for another five or six years.

Debt is a massive problem in our society. Statistics show that one in three people are 'black listed' because of the debt they've incurred. Ex-partners involved in 70 per cent of broken marriages cite financial difficulties as the main reason for the marital breakdown. One in four household arguments revolve around disputes over money. Those who find themselves caught in the debt trap face overwhelming experiences of stress, fear, isolation and helplessness. I regularly see people fall apart emotionally over the pressure that it causes.

There are a number of causes for a debt crisis, including the easy availability of credit. In the past, people would have saved before making a purchase, but today they are more likely to buy now and pay later. At the same time, our perceived needs have changed and people feel that they have the right to buy luxury goods and designer products for themselves. There is a sense in which our identities have become defined by what we have. You look at television programmes like *Who Wants to Be a Millionaire* and *The National Lottery* and there is a real 'get-rich-quick' ethos without any work involved. This whole idea is sold as the answer to our problems because to get rich is to get happy. It is one of the biggest and most successful lies that we have fallen for, because all the evidence shows that consumerism does not bring happiness. Divorce and suicide rates are overwhelmingly higher among the rich than any other sector in our society.

The problem is exacerbated by the tendency of some companies to take advantage of those who are vulnerable. I remember one elderly gentleman aged 80 who came to us for help. He had fought for his country as a fighter pilot in the Second World War and later worked at Tower Bridge in London. He had retired on a state pension, when his beloved wife of many decades died. Within two or three days of her death there was a knock at the front door and a man sponsored by a well-known bank said, 'We understand that your wife has died and we know how much you loved her and will want to do your best by her. We can arrange a wonderful funeral. We know that you cannot afford it so we have made arrangements to grant a loan on your house and all you have to do is to sign here.' Within a short space of time he had signed himself up to £18,000 of debt. No one bothered to explain the implications properly to him or to check whether he could actually afford the repayments. In fact, it was completely impossible for him to pay off the interest let alone the capital sum. The bank would simply repossess the house once he defaulted on his payments or died. He came to us desperate for help five months later. Fortunately, we managed to help him, but only after threatening to publicise the case. It is amazing the way in which a supposedly reputable company can take advantage of such a situation.

Another problem is the absence of adequate help for those caught in debt. Where I live, there is a waiting list of about 14 weeks to receive advice on debt from the Citizens Advice Bureau. In practical terms, someone who has received a court summons or has the bailiffs knocking on the door to seize their assets cannot wait for such help – they need it immediately. But even where help is available it can be very expensive. In the worst case scenario, a person who visits a specialist agency (though not the CAB!)

will be asked to pay a fee of up to £3,000 before a word has been said. And these are people who need advice because they have no money! On top of that, they will have to pay about 25 pence to the agency for every pound given to a creditor in settlement. A number of agencies are springing up and making big profits in this way because debt is such a big growth area.

Debt is a problem that can afflict anyone regardless of background or circumstance. The emotions that people experience – the stress, the guilt, the fear, the feeling of failure and the sleepless nights – are the same whether the debt is a few hundred pounds or hundreds of thousands of pounds. We get people from all social backgrounds. We've had people who have been high fliers in the city when something has happened: maybe they have become unwell or their business has collapsed, or their marriage has broken down and there are now two households rather than one to pay for.

My own encounter with debt made me realise how little support there is for those who struggle with such issues. Talking about money is a social taboo, and when people asked me how I was, I knew they didn't really want to know the answer. When we did admit to having financial difficulties people would say glibly, 'Oh yes, so are we!' Trying to get them to understand the depth of the problem was very difficult. It wasn't much better in the church, where all too often we did not find the kind of support we needed.

The climate of fear, ignorance and social shame surrounding debt made me want to do something about it. I couldn't see any way to improve the situation other than talking about the issues and providing a forum for others to be heard. I wanted to explode the issue of debt in the church, because it is so important and we should be taking it seriously. Throughout the Old and New Testament there are frequent references to money. One in every 16 verses in the New Testament relates to money and possessions. If you can't have open and honest discussions about your financial circumstances in the church, then you can't have them anywhere.

I was at a prayer meeting in our church one Sunday evening, sitting in the corner on my own, when I suddenly heard God say audibly, 'Your vision is not wide enough: I want you to take this out beyond the church into the community.' I felt him impress on me that I mustn't wait any longer but must do it there and then. I did not need to wait until I was old enough or qualified enough. I was amazed because I had never heard God speak to me like that before. But, at the very next moment, one of our elders came over to me and said, 'God has been talking to you and you need to be obedient!' It was all the impetus I needed to get on with the job!

The first thing I did was to look around and see if there were any other models of churches offering debt advice to the community. I came across a few general advice centres dealing with things like AIDS and marital problems, but I couldn't find any that dealt specifically with debt. I therefore looked at the models provided by secular agencies and tried to draw upon the good practice while discarding the bits that I felt were unsuitable. I decided to set up a centre where people who had nowhere else to turn could come and be heard and find practical help in negotiating with their creditors. The advice would be free because I did not want to make a profit out of those who were already in financial distress.

After six months of preparation, we opened the doors of our Community Debt Advice Centre in April 1997. Our first clients came by invitation through local churches. We also had leaflets printed, and placed some in the local library, the job centre and distributed others in solicitors' offices and doctors' surgeries. We also advertised in the Yellow Pages and were recommended by the Citizens Advice Bureau. We have had an amazing response from people all over the South East, with somewhere in the region of 300 clients having come through the door and another 250 having been helped by telephone. We regularly see new people each week, so life is very busy as one client can generate as much as 20–25 hours' work.

Our usual opening hours are Monday evenings, Tuesday mornings (for administration) and Wednesday daytime. We have a team of volunteers ready to see clients. Technically we are a drop-in centre, but most people prefer to ring to make an appointment. The first meeting with a client is very informal over a cup of coffee. The aim is to build up a picture of what is going on. We need to establish if there are any emergencies that need to be addressed straight away. The clients are asked to sign a simple contract to protect our legal position. Otherwise, we just listen to them because that is what many of them need. We often need a box of tissues because debt is a very emotional subject for people to talk about. Alternatively, the pain sometimes comes out in anger as clients get rid of frustrations and express feelings of having been unfairly treated. It is a question of knowing how to handle their pain without taking it personally. Our aim is to build up a relationship of trust. After all, our clients are talking to a complete stranger about the intimacies of their financial affairs. I don't think I would particularly enjoy doing it! So we have to make it as easy as possible.

When we meet the client again, we need to clarify their finances. It can be as simple as calculating their total income, expenditure and debt. After subtracting all their reasonable expenses, we determine how much disposable income is left over to pay the creditors. We distinguish their priority debts – those that carry significant consequences, such as imprisonment or the loss of utilities (for example, electricity and gas), or where bailiffs are threatening to come in. We attempt to negotiate a package agreement with the creditors, making sure that all the priority debts are covered first. Where there is not much disposable income it will only be possible to pay a small amount per month and therefore the package can carry on for years.

It is very common for people to have no idea of the extent of their debt. I remember one husband and wife who came in and said they had about £20,000 of debt. But as we started writing down each company that they owed money to the list grew and grew. When I added all the debts up, they came to in excess of £170,000! Of course, in situations like that you have to be very sensitive about how you break the news to the clients. Fortunately, in that case they were able to sell their house and move to a smaller one and pay off all their debts over a five-year period.

Other clients only reveal the true extent of their situation over time. I have a number of clients who come back three or four months later and say, 'I have just discovered this Visa bill.' There is one gentleman who has done this to me seven times! It was difficult for him to admit that he had got into such a mess and so he found it easier to confess it bit by bit. We have to be careful because we need to gain the trust of the creditors and it's difficult to do this when you have to keep renegotiating because of new information. But on the other hand, this particular man was learning to trust us over time. If I had turned around and said, 'Why didn't you tell me? Now you have wrecked our relationship with the creditors,' he would have been humiliated and wouldn't have come back again.

It is an important principle of the centre that we encourage people to acknowledge their role in the problem, and our approach differs from many agencies in this respect. For example, we will not visit the client but insist that they make the effort to come to our office for help. Similarly, we are quite clear that it is the client's responsibility to ensure that the agreed payments are made, and it is not our job to oversee the process. And we encourage our clients to take responsibility for the debts that they owe. One client I remember learnt the hard way when he went to prison for six months for refusing to pay council tax. On his release, not only was he still obliged to pay the debt, but it had increased because his wife had been living in the house in the meantime! Some agencies will use any loophole to help their clients escape from what they owe. However, I believe that if the client has the financial means, then he or she is morally obliged to pay what is fair. Even if it takes them a long time, they will ultimately feel more empowered when they manage to discharge their responsibilities themselves.

One of the distinctive things about the centre is the way in which it is connected to Burgess Hill Community Church. The two are wrapped up together. Our offices are in the church building and we are part of their integral structure. Without the church the centre would not exist. The church has a membership of about 100 adults. We are just one of the projects they run on behalf of the community. For example, they also run marriage resource counselling and courses on practical parenting. They also have a Mums and Toddlers group which runs on the same day as the Debt Advice Centre so that if our clients have children they can be looked after downstairs.

We are funded entirely by the Community Church. They give us an annual budget of £2,400, out of which we cover all our costs. Occasionally we receive one-off gifts or specific grants from people, but we don't solicit them. We originally tried applying for funding from the local council, but they responded that they would rather give their money to the Citizens Advice Bureau! The CAB themselves viewed us as a threat for a while, but now we have developed quite a good relationship with them, and they realise that our combined work is still not enough to meet all the needs in the community. Our relationship with the local council is mixed. We work well with the departments responsible for housing benefit and council tax benefit, and they have given us direct telephone numbers to access information. But the council's general view of us is suspicious.

Another distinctive fact about the Community Debt

Advice Centre is that all the staff are volunteers. At the moment we have ten, all from Burgess Hill Community Church and the Kings Church in Haywards Heath. We have invited other local churches to help out with volunteering if they would like to. Our volunteers are not involved professionally in this area. The best debt advisers are those who can listen. They do not need to be experts in finance. We have people from all sorts of backgrounds, including a farmer, a double-glazing salesman, a couple of PR people and a teacher. We are just ordinary people who are interested in other ordinary people.

None of the volunteers had any formal qualifications in finance before we started. Welfare provisions can be very complicated. So we undertook some training with Birmingham Settlement, and then we organised six evenings where people came to give us talks. Many of them were people from the congregation or other churches, who worked in a related area and could teach us something about it. For example, we had a lawyer to explain the court system, someone from the Job Centre to talk about employment and a counsellor to teach us how to listen. We also put ourselves through the Social Services benefits programme. Ultimately, you can never be trained in every area for debt advice. The proper training starts when you are hands-on doing it.

Listening is the key element, and this is one area where we are different to any other agency that I know. Most agencies will simply grant a fixed period interview of, say, 45 minutes, regardless of the complexity of the case or the needs of the client. I believe that it is so important to give people who have bravely taken the first step in admitting their situation the time to talk about their problems and the impact it is having on their lives. We must never focus solely on the financial details to the exclusion of the person sitting in front of us. I remember one lady who came to us for advice but just started crying for an hour and a half – all we could do was to hand her tissues and a cup of coffee! At the end of her outpouring, although we had really achieved very little in terms of addressing the financial problem, she stood up and said, 'Thank you, I feel so much better now.' That is a big part of what we are about. We have the luxury of being different because we don't have to worry about meeting targets or being profitable. Our aim is to build relationships. It is to show that we genuinely care and that we are there for our clients. That is why it is not just about being debt advisers, it is about being the church.

The work can be very painful. Some of the situations you are encountering are very distressing for you as well as for the client. Sometimes you come out of an interview and all you want to do is bash your head against the wall because you feel so angry. Sometimes this is because the client is so rude. It is important to have a good team around who can give support without judging you. We always end by praying together as a team so that we do not go home carrying the weight on our own.

Some people wonder why a church should get involved in debt advice. I would not be doing it if I wasn't a Christian and I didn't know Jesus in the personal way that I do. It is only because of the way in which we have experienced the love of God that we can show love to others. Historically, it was the churches who were responsible for a good deal of welfare and looking after the needy. It wasn't until the last century, when the welfare state and NHS really evolved, that the churches shed their sense of responsibility. Yet one of our biggest callings above anything else is to be out there in society, affecting it and having an impact through serving it. I am not doing this to make myself feel better. I am doing this because the Bible clearly says we should. In the Old Testament, God judged the Israelites for not taking their responsibility to help the poor, the needy and the widows seriously. This is echoed through what Jesus taught in the New Testament. I particularly love Luke 4:16 where Jesus picks up the scroll in his local synagogue and says God anointed him to bring good news to the poor and to bind up the broken-hearted. This is the heart of God. You cannot escape it unless you read the Bible with a closed heart.

Some people say debt counselling is a distraction from evangelism. But what is evangelism? Evangelism is actually being a light to the community. It means showing an alternative way of living. If you set a good example, then people will want to know why. The first question of all our clients is 'Do you charge?'. When we say no, we go on to explain that the church funds us. Sometimes that leads them to ask us more questions and sometimes it doesn't. We have had clients come to Alpha courses, home groups and our church worship services through their contact with the Debt Advice Centre. But that is not our primary purpose. We are doing it because it is what we have been asked to do. Nothing more than that.

At the moment I am busy trying to develop new resources to deal with debt. I am writing manuals for teenagers, students and adults on money management. Recently, the New Frontiers initiative 'ACT 2000' sponsored us to write a training manual. The aim is to equip local churches to get out in the community without making the mistakes we did. Consequently, we have been involved in helping 18 new centres get started in the last 18 months based on the model in Burgess Hill. They are free to take on board any of our ideas and to discard what they don't think will be of any use.

Every one of our advisors would say that once you get into debt advice you cannot stop. To see the change in people's lives is so rewarding. A couple of years ago someone asked what my vision was and I said it was for every single church in the UK to have at least one person trained up in debt advice. But I have since changed my mind. Now I want it to go out around the world. The model is so simple and transferable to any society – it couldn't be easier. And yet it couldn't be more important or exciting!

Relevant contacts

The Community Debt Advice Centre has, with the help of Act 2000 (New Frontiers International), produced an accessible guide to 'Setting up a Debt Advice Centre'.
12 Mill Road
Burgess Hill
West Sussex
RH15 8DR
Tel: 01444 232 444
Email: enquiries@debtadvicecentre.com
www.debtadvicecentre.com

Birmingham Settlement provides training to develop the skills and resources of community-based organisations.
318 Summer Lane
Birmingham B19 3RL
Tel: 0121 248 3000
www.birminghamsettlement.org.uk

Credit Action provides a wide range of materials, speakers and courses.
6 Regent Terrace
Cambridge CB2 1AA
Tel: 01223 324 034 / Freephone debt helpline: 0800 591 084
Email: credit.action@dial.pipex.com
www.creditaction.com

Money Advice Association provides training and support for new money advice projects.
Kempton House
Kempton Way
Dysart Road
Grantham NG31 7LE
Tel: 01476 594 970
Email: maa@mail.bogo.co.uk
www.maa.ndirect.co.uk

3. Higher Force Challenge, Belfast

Jack McKee is the pastor of the New Life Fellowship in the divided Shankill community in West Belfast. He has developed a number of community initiatives, but in this chapter we focus on the Higher Force Challenge programme he started in 1992. The aim of the project is to work with young people at risk of being drawn into a life of unemployment, drug abuse, crime and paramilitary violence. Although based in a Protestant area, the programme initiates cross-community work between Catholics and Protestants. Jack's work has brought him into direct contact with all the major paramilitary organisations, and he has been subjected to a series of threats and acts of violence. Jack is 48, and married to Kathleen. Their three children are all adults.

Andy Johnson was an active member of our youth group in the North Shankill area of Belfast. I had known him for a number of years, and he was a committed Christian. One day, when he was aged 17, he was watching the news and it was reported that five Catholic people had been shot dead not far from where he lived. As he witnessed the scenes and saw the pain and heartache caused, he fell on the floor weeping. He cried out to his mother, 'Why do people do this in the name of Protestantism? How can they claim to do this for God when it is nothing but blatant murder?'

A few evenings later, Andy was working in a video rental shop. Just a hundred yards away his friends in the youth group were meeting at our church. While they were worshipping God, a car pulled up outside his shop. Two men stepped out of the car with guns and came through the shop door. They opened fire and Andy was hit twice in his chest. He died on the shop floor. It was a tit-for-tat killing for the very deaths that he had wept over just a few days before. He was the victim for no reason other than he was a Protestant in the wrong place at the wrong time.

I live and work in a divided community, and it is not just a case of the animosity between Catholics and Protestants. Today, the Protestant factions are warring between themselves. Sadly, even churches are divided against each other. The escalation of fear and crime is robbing the community of its life. Just a couple of weeks ago, another young man I'd worked with was killed so violently that his body was unrecognisable. How is a pastor supposed to respond in these kinds of circumstances? As a Christian, how can I minister the true love and hope of God in a place like the Shankill community?

I was born in 1952 and brought up in the Shankill area. In my early days I grew up with Catholic neighbours and friends without any problems. Although there were political disputes dating back to the partition of Northern Ireland in 1921, it was not until the civil rights marches of the 1960s that the troubles, as we now know them, began. In 1969 a march was organised by a group connected with the Orange Order. As they walked around the walls of Derry, they were stoned and petrol-bombed by Catholic groups, and the Protestant community rose up in retaliation.

The violence escalated right across Belfast. People were being killed on a daily basis and hundreds of homes were being burned out as the two communities turned against each other. We initially thought that the fighting would be short-lived, but the sad reality is that it has now lasted for over 30 years. The Shankill Road area soon became the major flash-point for the troubles. And as it became apparent that the violence was going to continue, it was decided to separate the Protestant and Catholic communities. In some parts of west Belfast, Catholics were moved to the Falls Road side and Protestants to the Shankill Road area. Finally, a wall was put up between the two communities; a wall still exists today.

The Shankill Road has become a highly symbolic centre for Protestant loyalism, with the result that all the Protestant paramilitary organisations have based themselves here. Although these groups have organised themselves right across Northern Ireland, they are still firmly controlled from their bases within the Shankill area. Twenty years ago the population of the Shankill community was about 67,000, but today it has dropped drastically to around 25,000 and is still falling. This decline in population is partly a reflection of the impact of the ongoing troubles and partly the result of redevelopment and upward mobility.

It is often claimed that the conflict is over religion: Protestantism versus Catholicism. However, that kind of analysis fails to understand the root of the real problem. It is true to say that Catholics and Protestants have been fighting each other for the past three hundred years, but in reality people are not at war over their religious beliefs, but rather their political and territorial claims. The reason Protestant loyalists went to war was to fight for what they regard as 'the British way of life'. Today, I would be surprised if as many as 8 per cent of the 'Protestant' community in the Shankill area even attend church.

Self-interest and racketeering have also become significant factors to add to the problems of the community, as paramilitary groups have sought to establish their own power bases and to control and manipulate the communities on both sides of the wall. This was recently evidenced on the Shankill Road when a feud broke out in August 2000 between the UVF (Ulster Volunteer Force) and the UFF (Ulster Freedom Fighters). Before it was settled, seven people were dead, dozens were wounded and literally hundreds were either forcibly moved or had little choice but to leave their homes because they were associated with the wrong paramilitary group. We had to physically help many of them take their furniture out of their homes, and bring it down to our church for storage. Many of the houses are still boarded up today.

The Shankill community is one of the most deprived communities in the whole of Europe. Unemployment is at around 17 per cent, and among young people it is as high as 35 per cent. Most young people leave school without any educational qualifications and end up on the New

Deal Scheme for employment training. After six months
they are back on the dole with no prospect of employment.
This in turn leads to huge boredom and the absence of any
long-term plans or vision. Many young men end up standing around on street corners from morning to night with
nothing else to do and nowhere else to go. Meanwhile,
young girls sit around at home and spend their day watching television or playing video games. Teenage pregnancy
is a big problem, there is a high crime rate, and many of
the kids turn to drugs at a young age. In fact, we have even
had to work with children as young as eight who have
been taking drugs. Even worse, a number of these kids are
trapped by the controlling organisations into becoming
dealers, simply because a young boy aged 14 standing on a
street corner is less likely to be harassed by the local police
than an adult. The big-time drug dealers are not going to
expose themselves and so are quite happy to bring in
young lads to deal for them at the cost of a few pounds or
some free drugs at the end of the week. These are the kinds
of kids that we have made it our goal to reach through our
Higher Force Challenge programme.

I went to Bible College in South London for two years in
1979. Prior to that I had spent five years in the UDR (the
Ulster Defence Regiment), which at the time was the
largest regiment in the British army made up almost exclusively of people from Northern Ireland. I joined because I
wanted to do something about the troubles, but as a new
Christian I knew that terrorism was wrong. Many of my
friends were killed at this time. One close friend was shot
dead in his own home in front of his child. I found myself
the subject of an attempted murder. I was shot at five times

by a gunman just 30 feet away from me. Miraculously, all five shots missed and I survived. Shortly afterwards I was informed by the police that I was on the IRA death list. One night, some time later, I was disturbed by a sound at three o'clock in the morning, and as I peeped out of the bedroom window I saw two men placing a bomb under my car. In all these events, I came to see God's hand of protection upon my life. However, today there is still an ongoing personal price to pay for my work in terms of my own sense of safety, and I have received death threats from both major paramilitary organisations within the Protestant community.

On returning from Bible College, I began to pastor an Elim Pentecostal church 35 miles south of Belfast. I was there for two-and-a-half years, and then in 1982 was given the opportunity to move to a church back where I had grown up – in the Shankill Road community. Things went well there, but by 1989 we started to feel unsettled because we didn't feel we were doing enough as a church to reach the needs of the youth in the Shankill community. This was a time of increased intensity in the paramilitary movement, and there was an upsurge of punishment beatings and shootings. A very prevalent problem at that stage was 'knee-capping': the shooting of young men in the knees to blow their knee caps off their legs. The damage done was not only physical to the immediate victim, but psychological in terms of the whole community, bringing with it a sense of domination and control by the local paramilitary groups.

I began to question the ethos of my ministry. My aim had always been that people would come to our church at

6.30 on Sunday evenings to listen to us sing and hear me preach. It slowly dawned on me that not only was this not happening, but even worse, that it was never going to happen. In fact I realised that people were staying away from our church in their thousands. So I began to search the Bible to discover some Scriptural basis for the way I was pastoring my church. Through that process, I realised I couldn't find one single verse that commanded the world to come to church. But what I did find was the verse that commanded the church to go into the world and preach the gospel. This challenged me so deeply that I knew I had to begin to find opportunities to take what we were doing out and to begin to work with young people on the streets.

However, what we needed was a practical vehicle to do that. One day, while I was praying about all this, my wife was reading the local newspaper in the living room. I remember that she suddenly called out to me, 'Jack, the Stadium is for sale.' The Stadium was a cinema on the Shankill Road, and for the next few days I just couldn't get that statement 'the Stadium is for sale' out of my mind. However, at the same time, I couldn't think what possible use it would be to us as a church. Then I slowly began to see that maybe it could provide exactly the link into the community we had been searching for, and so I eventually decided to put in a bid.

While I was working as an 'ordinary' pastor in the community I never had any problems with the paramilitaries. But the moment I began to try and get the church to identify and align itself with the community, I began to run up against them. Having put in my bid for the Stadium, I was informed that one of the paramilitary groups wanted to buy it for their own reasons and I was 'advised' that I should not get in their way. They told me they were planning to put in an offer of £85,000, so I carefully explained that ours was not even worth half as much, at a mere £40,000. At the same time, I learnt that the Strand Cinema Company were talking about making an offer of £120,000. Imagine our surprise, then, when our bid was the successful one! Looking back, the reason was probably because our proposal for the use of the building was most in line with the aims of Belfast City Council who owned it. We were doubly excited when another government department gave us £20,000 towards the purchase price and a further £12,000 to help with the refurbishment.

Once we had purchased the Stadium, we were able to really get started on developing youth programmes and projects in the community. As a pastor I became more involved in twelve months with people at ground level in the community than I had in the previous twelve years. Though I continued to pastor the church until 1992, as the workload grew I eventually felt that it was time to move on and give myself full time to the community and youth projects that we were developing.

Over time we built up good relationships with young people in the community. We would run all sorts of projects, including concerts and clubs for pool, snooker, table tennis, indoor football and so on. We built an assault course inside the Stadium and knocked a couple of offices together to make a cafeteria so that the kids had somewhere to meet off the street. The Stadium is a focal building in the community, and was itself quite a good attraction for the young people. They used to come off the streets to have a cup of coffee with us, and the trust that was established was incredible. We put on some gospel concerts, and through these events and personal evangelism we saw a good number of young people make commitments to Christ.

Our next task was to encourage them to get into a local church. At that point I had no intentions of starting another church myself. The Shankill Road is one-and-a-half miles long and already had over 40 churches. The last thing it needed was another one! However, we began to find that the young people couldn't settle in the existing churches. Unfortunately a lot of the congregations were made up almost exclusively of older people, who just could not cope with the kind of youth that we were seeing become Christians.

It was during this time I went to a conference in Jerusalem, and through a conversation there began to get excited about the idea of starting a different sort of church back in Belfast, specifically to cater for youth. I typed the vision up and presented it to my denominational board, who after some discussion agreed that we could start a new church out of the Stadium. We eventually launched 'New Life Fellowship' in 1993 and twelve people came along on the first night. Today there are 120 members who are fully committed both to the church and its vision within the community. People have come in and been blown away by the atmosphere. We have seen guys from para-military backgrounds in both the UVF and the UFF give all that up and totally dedicate their lives to serving Christ. Currently, even though I still serve as the senior pastor of the church and so am regularly preaching and pastoring, a huge focus for me has become the running of the Higher Force Challenge programme.

Higher Force Challenge is an eight-week programme, which primarily works with young people at risk in the Shankill community. We run three programmes per year with twelve kids each time. Each programme runs Monday to Friday, and from 9.00 a.m. (when we start with breakfast) to 4.00 p.m. Though our main target group is 16–26-year-old young men, we have occasionally also run programmes for younger people (such as difficult pupils at school) and older ex-prisoners.

We recruit participants through the clubs that we run and our other activities on the streets. Most of those who come on the programme are at risk due to low educational achievement, high levels of unemployment, anti-social behaviour or drug and alcohol abuse. Many have been caught up in the paramilitary violence. Some have already been recruited by paramilitary organisations, and others will certainly be considering it. A number of them have been the victims of paramilitary violence, having been shot, knee-capped or badly beaten. I remember one young man who had been shot in his ankles, knees and elbows all at the same time. Over the years, I have often approached paramilitary groups to try to get them not to punish a particular young person or not to force them to leave the country – sometimes with more success in this than others.

For young people within any community in Belfast there is the constant pressure to become involved with the paramilitaries, whether it is the IRA, the UVF, the UFF or whoever. The choice of group is normally determined by the community that the young person lives in. Some manage to resist the pressure, but the consequence is often that they become loners in the community – so sadly most eventually sign up. Terrifyingly, a person as young as 13 or 14 will sometimes become the commander of a group of 40 or so other young people.

The Higher Force Challenge programme is designed to help its participants become positive contributors to the life of the Shankill community rather than part of its problem. We work to achieve this by helping to give young people a better understanding of, and respect for, themselves, their community, and the cultural differences across the sectarian divide. Our aim is to get them to the point where they are able to plan for their own future. Most of them have never had the chance to think carefully about what they want to achieve in their lives.

The course is divided into morning and afternoon sessions. In the mornings we look at life issues. For example, we explore topics such as drugs, violence, sectarianism, health and education. The aim is to teach those with whom we are working how to make good choices and to take responsibility for their actions. The afternoons are taken up with more physical activities, such as go-carting or parachuting. Each course also has two residential trips further afield. One is in Northern Ireland and the other is either in England, Scotland or Wales.

Our annual budget is now nearly £200,000, and we raise most of our funds from sources such as the Probation Service (with whom we work in partnership), the International Fund for Ireland, Smiths Charity, Youth

Net, Children In Need and other peace and reconciliation agencies.

We forged links with the Probation Service because so many of the kids with whom we were working were involved in crime and other anti-social behaviour. I have to say that on the first programme, after we had finally convinced Probation to work with us, the Deputy Chief Probation Officer said that if we could manage to keep just two out of the twelve participants for the full eight weeks, then he would consider it to have been very successful. My response to him was that if at the end of the eight weeks we only had two on the programme I would never do it again! In fact, eleven out of the twelve who started the course completed it. And that sort of level of success has continued ever since.

In 1995 we began to launch cross-community projects with Catholics and Protestants, which has certainly proved to be a huge challenge. One of the things that is unique about our approach is that we run these courses in Belfast. Most cross-community programmes take place in Holland or America, because there is a perception that if you take the young people out of their environment, then they are more likely to relate to each other. While there is obviously a certain amount of truth in that philosophy, the problem is that when you bring them back home they usually lose all contact with each other. So we bring young men and women from the Catholic communities onto the Shankill Road, and take the Protestant kids into the Catholic areas. We work with similar clubs in Catholic communities such as Ardoyne, and have developed good relationships with their leaders. It is amazing to see how quickly trust and friendship has been built up, particularly as the Ardoyne and Shankill communities have been at loggerheads for 30 years.

When a new course starts, we get the participants to talk about their expectations as individuals and as a group, and then ask them to formulate and sign a shared contract on that basis. They commit themselves to each other, the project, the leaders, the venue and the community. The point is to get them to take responsibility for their own actions during the programme. Through formulating the contract, they are defining what they want to do for themselves. They also make a signed commitment that they will endeavour to stay on the programme for the full eight weeks and to participate in all the activities. This means that if any one of them steps outside the boundaries of the contract, then we are able to remind them of the commitment they made.

The course normally ends with a presentation day when we award certificates for completing the programme and for specific achievements, such as parachuting and canoeing. For many of these young men these are the first certificates that they have received for anything in their lives. I remember one young man who came to us in 1995. He was from a Protestant paramilitary background and passionately hated Catholics. The first time he ever came face to face with a Catholic in his life was on our programme. But over time they struck up a great relationship and that has continued to this day. When he finished the course his parents came along to the presentation day and said that this was the only time they could remember being at a public occasion with their son that wasn't in a court of law.

To date over 300 people have come through the programme. We have seen real changes in many of their ambitions and lives. We remain in contact with our previous participants through the Higher Force Challenge Club, which runs twice a week on similar principles to the programme, except that it is entirely optional. It combines a mix of fun activities with group discussion and training. I would estimate that we are still in regular contact with at least half of those who have been on the Higher Force Challenge over the last eight years. Many of them have left the problems of their youth behind, and a good number have settled down and are playing a really positive role in the life of their community.

Barry Stephens is a good example of the kind of success we have seen. Barry was one of the participants in our second programme. He came from a background of paramilitary involvement and drug abuse. He had just made a commitment to Christ when he joined us, and we were able to give him the opportunity he needed for a new start. He had left school at 15 years of age with no educational qualifications whatsoever. He had absolutely no belief in himself at all. But the Higher Force Challenge had a huge impact on him, and today it is true to say that he is a completely different person. After completing the course, he stayed on with us as a volunteer, during which time he went on to complete a twelve-month IT course. He then remained with us for a further four years as a volunteer instructor, even though we could only pay him £45 a week expenses on top of his dole money. Then, three years ago, we managed to access funds for a proper salary through European funding. Today, Barry is not only a key member of our full-time staff, but has gone on to gain a number of impressive qualifications. For example, he has become a qualified youth worker with the Belfast Educational Library Board. He has also completed an 18-month course at a university in Belfast to gain a diploma in Youth and Community Work. He is now well known and respected across the community and is a great asset to us. He is a brilliant role model, and, in fact, a number of other community groups have now invited him to sit on their boards to help them with some of the issues they are facing.

There is a lot of Christian content in the Higher Force Challenge programme, but it is more covert than overt. Although three of our staff are committed Christians, we do not push our faith on anyone. Our platform to preach comes through the church. New Life Fellowship is heavily involved in evangelism in the community, as well as within the building. However, we have to distinguish between people's primary needs and ultimate need. Sometimes the primary need is to be fed, and so our goal is to feed them – nothing less, nothing more. We do not have a right to get them to resolve their ultimate need before we are prepared to meet their primary needs with no strings attached.

Life still holds many challenges. For instance, we recently came under significant pressure to sell our building on to a wider community partnership. We eventually agreed to this because we were guaranteed the right to continue our work there. However, in practice it has now become virtually impossible for us to make this relationship work, because of the levels of rent being charged. Fortunately we have found other premises we can make use of at the moment, and we are now actively thinking about where we go in the future.

The key motivating factor behind all I do in the community is my personal commitment to Christ. I believe that if Jesus were in Northern Ireland today, he would be out in the community with the people and not just sitting in a church building somewhere. It is my belief that the great need for the church in this country is to wake up to its responsibility. I often make the point that the Bible does not say in 2 Chronicles 7:14 'if the politicians, or if the paramilitaries, or if the people on the streets humble themselves', but 'if my people, who are called by my name, will humble themselves and pray and seek my face and turn from their wicked ways, then will I hear from heaven and will forgive their sin and will heal their land'. This suggests to me that the church has an awesome responsibility when it comes to the healing of the land. Rather than focusing on the things that divide and separate us, we should be exploring ways in which we can work together.

So what is my ongoing personal vision? I believe that despite the troubles of the last 30 years, God is at work in the Shankill community, and so it is worth his people investing in it too. My dream is that one day Shankill may be an example to the world of the reconciliation God can bring to a divided area. I know that it will take a miracle, but God is a God of miracles, and I have been privileged to see one or two of them already.

Relevant contacts

Elim Pentecostal Church provides general consultation and support to churches.
PO Box 38
Cheltenham
Gloucestershire GL50 3HN
Tel: 01242 519 904
www.elim.org.uk

Oasis Trust runs mentoring projects and provides degree-accredited training for youth and community workers.
115 Southwark Bridge Road
London SE1 0AX
Tel: 020 7450 9000
Email: postmaster@oasistrust.org
www.oasistrust.org

YMCA has 150 years' experience of helping young people build a future. It offers guides, manuals and expertise in working with young people.
YMCA England
640 Forest Hill Road
London E17 3DZ
Tel: 020 8520 5599
www.ymca.org.uk

Youth for Christ offers support, training, materials and events to equip local churches to work with young people.
Church Resource Dept
PO Box 5254
Halesowen B63 3DG
Tel: 0121 550 8055
Email: yfc@yfc.co.uk
www.yfc.co.uk

4. The WIRE Project, Littlehampton

Paul Sanderson founded the WIRE in 1997. In a short period, it has brought a remarkable sense of community to a dispirited estate on the south coast of England. The project has been innovative in working with children and parents, and has among other things pioneered a radio station and an annual festival in the locality. Paul continues to manage the project which now employs 13 people. He is 33 years old and married to Heather. Together they have two sons aged six and two.

'Wick is a crap place to live and you can tell 'em I said so.' That is how one resident described Wick to me when I first arrived. Others called it 'a dumping ground; a dead-end place that you can't escape from.' Situated between the sea and the South Downs in Littlehampton, West Sussex, it is occasionally possible to glimpse something of the farming heritage of the area. But Wick is now a concrete island that is disconnected from wealthier suburbs by a dual carriageway and railway line. It is an estate that houses 7,000 people.

As an area of deprivation, Wick ranks badly compared to other parts of the south coast. Statistics reveal a huge number of needs caused by parenting issues, teenage pregnancies, mental health problems, crime, high unemployment, partners in prison and so on. The gates of the local school are the scene of regular arguments between parents who come to collect their children. The roads are peppered with disused cars, some that have been abandoned and burnt out. There have been attempts to improve the environment by planting trees, but the kids just pull them up. Some of the housing blocks have been renovated, but sadly it doesn't take long for them to fall back to their previous condition. And as I stood in Wick, even on my first day, I realised again that you have to do more than change the inside of a building to change a community – you have to change the inside of a person.

I've always loved doing voluntary work in the church, especially with children and after-school clubs. I enjoy making the children laugh and explaining Bible stories to them. In 1990 I decided to enrol on a year-long Christian leadership course called Training in Evangelism, run by Pioneer, the church network I belong to, in order to develop my skills with young people. Afterwards, I was fortunate enough to be employed by my home church in Surbiton, Surrey, as a community youth worker. During this time I set up a youth club called Reality on quite a rough estate. The kids used to turn up with their own pool cues ready for a fight. It could be a scary experience. I took on five or six volunteers to help out. And I started to recognise that not only did I enjoy working with kids, but I had an ability to draw others to exciting ideas and hear them say, 'I like this. I'll give it a crack too.'

At the same time, I began going back to my old school as a pastoral care worker three days a week. I was given my own room where young people could come and see me to talk through their issues. I was amazed at the response. They would often come before school, at lunch times and after school. I would just sit and listen to them. A lot of the time all they needed was two ears to hear the problems they faced, and then they would say, 'Oh I feel so much better now, thanks,' and off they would go. But the truth is sometimes I had to work very hard at listening, as it could get a bit boring, which is why I decided to go on some counselling courses to learn how to improve my skills.

I was still in the same job in 1996 when I got a phone call from the leader of Wickbourne Chapel, which is a church in Wick. He had been brainstorming with town counsellors, local businesses and local community members to see what could be done for their ward. They felt they needed a community worker: someone with vision, enthusiasm and ideas. In particular, they wanted someone with experience in basketball (which I had), counselling skills, youth clubs and schools work! My name was suggested, and the next thing I knew I was offered the job. 'We're going to get some money together, as we want to pay you to turn this community upside down,' they said. What an offer!

WIRE stands for Wick Information, Recreation and Education and its first office was a portacabin in the car park of Wickbourne Chapel. I began by researching the local area to find out what was going on. I arrived ready to change the world, but for three months I simply visited local schools, families and the local library to chat to people there in order to build my information about the area. At the time it was incredibly frustrating, but as I look back now I am very grateful for it. I used a questionnaire I had developed to discover what was good and what was bad about Wick, what the community needed and what the residents felt would make a positive difference. At the end of the three months I compiled my information into a report called 'What Makes Wick Tick' and sent a copy to everyone I could possibly think of. It outlined the community's strengths and weaknesses and the social problems its residents faced, as well as suggesting 13 different projects that I felt would really help to address the concerns and issues I'd heard expressed.

Rather than attempting to take on all 13 projects at once (which was a huge temptation!), I made the decision to prioritise, start with a couple and launch the others as soon as resources became available. The initial project we set up, called 'The Crew', began in 1997 after I met Jane. She arrived at my office, heavily pregnant, in a beaten-up old car that was untaxed. The father of her other four children was away in prison when she had conceived again. Pouring out her story she was desperate for my help.

I felt daunted, but I agreed to visit her home. As I walked into her flat the first thing to hit me was the dirt and the smell. I couldn't believe it. The windows were broken and the sofa had springs poking out of it and was covered in food and other muck. There were very few toys for the children. There were no wardrobes and all the clothes were kept in black bin-liners. There was no bed linen. A baby was lying on the floor with a bottle on a towel to keep it in its mouth. The conditions were appalling. But what I remember more than anything else was that the kids were so excited to have a visitor.

I just sat there and was overwhelmed by the pain, the poverty, and what I felt was the hopelessness of the situation. I wondered how I could possibly help to bring a family like that into some sense of healthy normality and hygiene. But the more we chatted, the more I began to realise that one of Jane's biggest problems was that she never had any time to herself. She was at her wits' end. It occurred to me that what she most needed was a break. So, almost without thinking, I said, 'How would you feel if I picked the kids up in my car once a week and we went out, so that you could have a bit of a breather?'

From then on every week I would pop in to say hello to Jane and then take the children down to the beach, up to the hills or to any other place that was local and free. Occasionally I would save up a fiver and take them swimming; something they loved but had never done before. And so it was from my involvement with Jane and her family that we developed The Crew. We now use a minibus to collect over 40 children each week and take them out for some fun after school. And we've seen the way in which it has helped to broaden their horizons, develop their self-esteem and confidence and give their parents a rest.

The second project we started was called the 'Teddy Tots' toddler group. There are hundreds of parents on the estate who spend most of their time alone stuck at home and who desperately need somewhere to go where they can engage socially with the rest of the community. We were able to get a crèche worker and some good toys for the children, so it didn't take much from there to create an environment at the chapel hall where we could sit down and chat with them. It costs us £6 for three days, which is about 90p per hour of child care.

In due course we started another project called the 'Live Wire Play Scheme' for those children who had outgrown Teddy Tots. These are high-energy gatherings of 200 or so kids (up to 350 in the summer when we hire a big marquee), which run in the school holidays from 10.00 a.m. to 12.30. p.m. It's really hard work and sometimes the kids are difficult, but when you see how it fits into the whole picture of the community's life it is so rewarding. The parents are keen, and when I go to school to drop my son off, the other children are for ever asking me, 'When's the next play scheme?'

We now run a number of other projects for children, such as our 'Breakfast Club' which takes place every morning in the local primary school. Our team go to give the kids a nutritional start to the day and to run some art and craft activities. The aim is to give a positive beginning to the day for many of these children who would otherwise start it without any breakfast or be late for school. Now they are punctual and have food in their stomachs, which, say the teachers, means they are more awake and ready for their education.

One of our favourite projects is 'Dance Nation'. It is a favourite because it is so easy to run. All you need is an instructor who can dance. The idea had already come from the community – so we just waited for the right leader to come along. Dance Nation presses all the right buttons with local agencies – exercise for kids is something that both government and health authorities want to encourage, so much so that they funded us. The local council gave us a £2,500 grant. We had actually only asked for £1,000 but they said they believed in us and they wanted to provide us with enough cash for a two-year start-up. We used the money to pay our instructor and also bought some quality equipment. However, we also charge £1 per child, per session, per week because, though we don't want to be seen as money-grabbers, we want to be responsible about teaching money management. However, if someone can't afford it we always make allowances.

The children at Dance Nation learn specific routines together. They watch *Top of the Pops* and then simply copy people like Britney Spears and Steps. At the end of the summer term we put on a show – and last year we also did nine or ten different school fêtes where Dance Nation performed – as well as our own festivals and Christmas pantomimes. We have even been on Saturday morning TV for the programme *Live and Kicking*, where our kids met Steps!

Halfway through every Dance Nation session we give the kids a short break. But instead of getting out the Coke cans and biscuits we teach them that nutrition is as important as physical exercise. So we provide a choice of some fruit, juices and milk and they are allowed to help themselves to as much as they like. Some weeks it's kiwi fruit or grapes and other times it's melon or a fruit cocktail! We know that if we can encourage them that it is trendy to eat fruit then they will nag their parents for more at the shopping centre and in the long run that will make a huge difference for them. And while they are munching away we chat as a group to get them to think about their dancing in relation to other lifestyle subjects such as smoking. What does smoking do to people who dance? What does it do to their muscles and lungs? We don't just say, 'Don't smoke because it is bad for you,' we talk about what it actually does do. We get them into groups and might have quizzes on nutrition, or perhaps examine skeletons that we have made to show how their bodies work. Of course the dancing is the attraction, but the kids go away after an hour at Dance Nation not only having done some great routines but also having learnt a lot more about themselves and developing a healthy lifestyle.

For the youth we run a number of projects including a nightclub and a scheme for teaching sex education that uses a computer programme to encourage teenage girls to think about the consequences of sex. For instance, 'The Mix' works with kids who are identified as being at risk of exclusion from the junior school. Educational 'exclusion' (it used to be called 'expulsion') is without doubt the start of social exclusion. Exclusion from school equals potential crime and drug involvement and huge problems in the future. We employ a youth worker who not only works with the kids but who makes a commitment to visit their parents at home every week, and meets their teachers once a month to talk through their progress. The aim is for the kids to collect points. If they regularly attend our after-school club, and if they go to school, they get points. They can also get points for team activities, community action, good school work, etc. Those who collect ten points in a two-week period get to go on a special outing. In the past we have done things like scuba diving, paintballing, go-karting, and rock climbing. All these activities are very special to them because it is such a deprived area. Our aim is to constantly show that good behaviour gets rewards, rather than to punish bad behaviour. A life principle is that behaviour that is rewarded will always be repeated – it actually applies to us all. The professionals say that it will take five years to see whether or not The Mix is effective, but some of the early feedback from parents and teachers is already very encouraging.

We have also begun to develop some work with parents. In fact, the Teddy Tots toddler group was specifically devised to enable us to build relationships with them and so overcome the distrust that they can often feel towards welfare agencies seeking to work with them. Not surprisingly, they resent being told how to parent their kids, and the thought of joining a course can easily feel like going back to school, from which some of them were originally excluded! However, through building personal relationships we have been able to slowly break those fears down.

It was six months after starting the toddler group that we were able to launch our first 'Surviving Parenthood' course. It looks at a variety of issues such as self-esteem, discipline, communication skills, different models of play and art and craft. And working with teenagers had taught me that communication through the teen years is a big issue, so we have also developed another course specifically on communicating with teenagers. I gathered material from here, there and everywhere to put them together. A lot of the original material was very middle-class and needed to be changed. For example, there is a pretty low literacy level in Wick so we have to be very careful about the level of wording we use and make sure that everything is read out loud. And an ice-breaker called 'Break into twos and talk about the best holiday abroad you've ever had' is not very appropriate for people who have hardly ever left Littlehampton!

We had eight mums come along to the first Surviving Parenthood course. Looking back, I was as nervous as they were and felt on top of the world when they came back again the following week! I talked through my notes, but they told their own stories and I slowly found I was learning a lot from them. My role was to facilitate. We provided the venue (the chapel building) and got together the material, the crèche worker and the tea and coffee. That is still the way it works. It is not 'go along to the WIRE and they'll teach you how to be a parent', it's an open forum where everyone learns from each other and we throw in some good tips and discussion starters. We don't give long talks. The content is put out through work sheets and a video. The parents work in pairs and debate the work sheet. Occasionally, we'll talk them through a particular technique and use role-plays, especially in the later weeks when they know each other better.

We have now had over 250 parents go through our parenting course, which has impacted people in all sorts of interesting ways we never expected. For example, when you get a mum coming in saying, 'I've got two kids and they are a nightmare – they tear around the house and give me a headache,' and then the next says, 'I'm a mum with four kids to bring up and my husband is in prison,' it helps the first mother to put her situation into perspective.

We make the courses fun and lively, but at times things

can also get very emotional. For instance, when you discuss the issue of a child's self-esteem it often raises the question of a parent's own sense of self-worth. In one case we had a mum come to us and say, 'From the age of four my mum regularly sat me down at night and said, "I wish you were never born" and still every night I hear those words echoing around in my head. Now I have my own three-and-a-half-year-old and I'm afraid of what I am. I'm afraid of what I feel. I don't want to say those same words, but I don't know any other way.' As she sat there and came out with that, other mums in the room just started to choke up. But over time we and the group were able to help her and the truth is that she's developed into a brilliant mum.

The success of Surviving Parenthood has encouraged us to develop a number of other projects for parents. For instance, we now offer IT training, which is very popular – we have a staff member who goes into homes (with a laptop computer paid for by the education authority!) to sit down with parents, some of whom have never touched a computer before, and teach them how to use it to write a letter. On the back of that, we also saw the need to make a trained financial advisor available to visit parents troubled with debt. We give them practical advice about handling money and how to budget. Wick has a big problem with loan sharks who prey on the vulnerable. I have been there when one of them has turned up to collect interest at 50 per cent on their loan. That kind of scenario is a nightmare for families who are already struggling financially. We know that every little step we take with any family to give them the financial skills they need makes a huge difference in the longer term.

And as we have built up relationships with parents on the estate, they have started to trust us to help them with other problems, including addictions. As for us, we are slowly gaining the confidence to deal with such problems as anger management, stress and alcohol abuse. For example, we have developed a course called 'Stub It Out' for people who want to give up smoking. Again, our first contacts came from Teddy Tots and Surviving Parenthood. If we had tried to run a Stub It Out group cold, no one would have turned up. Who would have trusted us to help them with such a personal issue?

People ask me where we get our course material from. We have gathered it by surfing the net, buying literature, going on training courses and even buying in the expertise. In the case of Stub It Out, the local health authority gives us an expert's time to run the course and our job is simply to facilitate it. But it's a real two-way street. The authorities work with us because they know that they would never be able to access these people without us!

God gave me a dream four years ago about Wick celebrating its community life by having a huge party. I shared my vision with some other local agencies and invited them to come in and help. This has now developed into an annual festival when, for seven days in the summer, we erect a marquee on the school playing field. We have play schemes and toddler groups in the morning, to which we invite guests such as doctors and police officers to talk to the families about their jobs. In fact, the district council has launched some of their key initiatives into the community at the festival because they know that is where they can best meet the people. In the afternoons we have football tournaments and youth events, as well as senior citizens' quizzes and bingo. In the evenings there are more quiz nights, youth events and off-site activities in pubs. We cram it all into seven days of hard work and energy, but it creates a lot of memories and people talk about the festival of Wick all year round.

Each year, as part of the festival, we run a community radio station called Wick FM. We get funding from a local business – it costs around £5,000 to run the station for two weeks. But for Wick to have its own radio frequency, with the whole of the estate waking up listening to their mates broadcasting, creates a massive community buzz. There are many problems still facing Wick, but without doubt the festival and the radio station have helped to foster a greater sense of community and pride in the area. I will never forget receiving a note saying, 'For the first time I am writing a letter with the word Wick in its address. For years I've been embarrassed to put that in my letters, but after the Festival of Wick and all that it has meant I am proud to live in Wick.'

Volunteers are a crucial part of WIRE's work, with over 200 involved last year. However, we are very careful to carry out police checks, take references and ensure safe procedures and supervision with all our volunteers who work with children, as one bad incident could ruin it for the whole project. We also place a great emphasis on train-ing our volunteers in communication skills, child behaviour management, child protection and first aid. We use ice-breakers and games to explore aspects of how to work with a child, or how to deal with an adult who is com-plaining. And then there's the question of how to answer a phone. A lot of people here answer the phone saying things like, 'Alright? What d'you want?' which is not so good if you have the Director of Social Services ringing you. So we teach them to say, 'Hello, my name is Dave. I work with the WIRE Project. How can I help you?'

Such training equips people not only for their present role at the WIRE, but also for the future. For instance, we had a mum who always wore dark glasses. She didn't like going out and kept herself to herself. But her son was in one of our projects which she really appreciated, and one day she offered to help. She was good with children and we told her so. As a result we trained her for one of the toddler group leadership teams. She loved the work and she started keeping the accounts and coming up with ideas for arts and crafts. You could see her confidence growing, and eventually she stopped wearing her dark glasses. She developed the toddler group in a way I never could have. After a few months she said, 'Paul, I am really sorry but I am going to have to leave. I've got a full-time job in nursing care.' What a transformation – six months before, she was sitting in her home isolated and unable to work, but we gave her the opportunity and she grabbed hold of it. That happens quite regularly. I often find myself writing references and helping young people write CVs as a result of the voluntary work they have done with us. And you can't believe what it feels like when someone comes back with a big smile on their face and announces, 'I got the job, I got the job!'

We also work as hard as we can to thank our volunteers, both verbally and by letter, for all they give. For instance, we present to young volunteers certificates, which go into their record of achievement. If a young person is committing themselves to four days of hard work with noisy kids for no money during their school holiday, they deserve recognition. We also give them a mug. They are not expensive but are well appreciated. In fact, the mugs end up in real places of honour in homes. People are quite proud of them.

I am often asked how I get volunteers. I would say I work hard to look after them and do all I can to create a memorable and enjoyable experience for them. I aim to give them responsibility, trust and respect. We have a voluntary support pack explaining job descriptions and opportunities. And we even offer an expense form, though nobody has ever claimed on it!

Another question I'm often asked by Christians is how our faith expresses itself. Of course, some Christians have accused us of not being evangelistic enough, while some local politicians and professionals think that we are far too Christian. It's a tough balance. The truth is, it's pretty hard to miss that we are Christians. We work out of Wickbourne Chapel, where there's a huge mural on the wall which states: 'Jesus is Lord!' All of our literature expressly states that the WIRE project is a practical expression of the Christian faith. We are not shy of our faith. For instance, some of the songs in our play schemes are Bible-based. The kids go home singing the songs and we've never had a complaint from a single parent about it. We did have a complaint from a town counsellor once, who thought it was inappropriate. I suggested that he asked the parents for their view and I never heard from him about it again! In my heart of hearts I am an evangelist, because I know that God has a desire for every human being to be in relationship with him.

We work with a number of agencies who are not Christians and we receive funding from secular organisations such as the local council and Children in Need. They lay down criteria that we cannot promote religious belief as a project, which we honour. Nonetheless, I believe that the boundaries are loose enough for us to express our Christian faith and understanding through our actions and lifestyles – which is, of course, the way we like it. The WIRE is actually a Spurgeon's Child Care project. Spurgeon's is a Christian foundation with a 130-year-long history. Someone once asked its founder, Charles Spurgeon, 'You have seen many saved and preached many sermons: what was the greatest sermon you have ever preached?' He replied, 'The greatest sermon I have ever preached has been the orphanages and the family homes I have set up.' I live by the same principle. Yes, words are important. There is a time in every relationship where trust has been built so that the word of the Lord can be preached, but it can take a long time to get there. I see the WIRE project as very much God's hand in the community, whether it's a shoulder to cry on if someone is grieving or mourning, or a party to celebrate with someone who has passed an exam, or a wedding or funeral where I hold someone's hand. My goal is to represent Jesus in all these situations.

When I read the Bible I see that Jesus created a place of belonging where the disciples, women and children felt they could be a part of something – where they were welcomed rather than pushed aside. The WIRE does that. People choose to come because they feel they belong. The church so often says, 'You can only belong once you believe.' I feel this is wrong theology that displays an attitude which really upsets God. We need to create 'belonging' and then pray and pray and pray for belief. I think it is appropriate to speak about my faith when people ask me questions, and I would say that every couple of weeks a question about my motivation or attitude creates a link for me to talk about the gospel.

At the end of one parenting course a mum told me how brilliant she had found it. She also explained that she was going to tell her friend who, she said, hadn't come along because she had thought that we would be getting the Bible out at the end of each week and forcing people to read it. She commented, 'You haven't done that and I appreciate it.' When she had gone, I paused and thought, 'Sorry Lord. *Should* I have got it out?' But then I realised that her need at that moment was not to have the Bible read to her. Of course I know that she did need the Bible, but at that precise moment her inability to handle her three-year-old kid was making her pull her hair out. That was the point at which she needed help. And she'd probably be back with her friend in tow!

Some of those we have worked with are now our key workers and volunteers and have become far more knowledgeable about the Bible and its message than they ever would have been if we had preached at them. They have seen us and walked alongside us and sometimes popped into church events that we have been at. The mum who thought we'd force the Bible on her did decide to come to the next parenting course. She then decided to send her daughter to the play group attached to Wickbourne Chapel, where they pray together. In fact, they now say grace together as a family and each day her daughter attends the church's after-school club. I hope that we play an important part in breaking down the negative stereotypes that people seem to have about the church.

My salary as Director of WIRE is funded by the government's Single Regeneration Budget. That means that it has to be matched, though not necessarily in cash, from elsewhere. However, the hours that our volunteers work are now worth over £60,000 a year. We have also received funding from Children in Need, the Local Health Authorities, West Sussex Social Services jointly with the Drug Action Team, Kelloggs (to assist with our breakfast club), and The Body Shop International. Local churches and individuals also give us around £5,000 a year and volunteers have raised funds on our behalf.

Sponsors are looking for partnerships which we provide. But the WIRE believes that as an expression of our Christian faith we need to work to turn our formal partnerships into deeper relationships and friendships. So we put effort into meeting socially with our sponsors, not to get more money out of them, but because we want a friendship with them. As a result we've found that in some cases their volunteers also help us out with some of our projects. We've also been invited to go to talk about our projects to their staff. Partnership is where it is at, but unfortunately the church has been guilty of a lone-ranger mentality for a lot of its history. The WIRE would not have got where it has without other people helping us, guiding us, being constructively critical and encouraging us when we get it right.

Of course, we have our ups and downs. Some partners have been difficult, which has been painful. Sadly, this has been true of some churches as much as anybody else. Someone once wrote to Spurgeon's Child Care asking if they were sure that I was really a Christian! However, what we are seeking to model at the WIRE is unity with other churches, businesses, Social Services, Health Authorities and counsellors. Together we believe that we can make a difference on this estate. Together we can change our neighbourhood for good.

Relevant contacts

Care for the Family produces practical resources to equip and inspire married couples, parents and children.
PO Box 488
Cardiff CF1 1RE
Tel: 029 2081 0800
Email: care.for.the.family@dial.pipex.com
www.care-for-the-family.org.uk

Family Care is an adoption agency and independent social work agency for families.
Warren House
2 Pelham Court
Nottingham NG5 1AP
Tel: 0115 960 3010
Email: family-care@bigfoot.com
www.family-care.demon.co.uk

Parentalk produces resources and training materials to inspire parents to enjoy parenthood.
115 Southwark Bridge Road
London SE1 0AX
Tel: 0700 2000 500
Email: info@parentalk.co.uk
www.parentalk.co.uk

Spurgeon's Child Care provides practical resources and consultancy to equip churches to work with children and young people.
Mr Hugh R. Minty
Freepost NH0229
Rushden
Northants NN10 9BR
Tel: 01923 412 412
Email: SCC@spurgeons.org
www.spurgeonschildcare.org

5. Family Matters, Luton

Trevor Adams is the Senior Pastor of the Church of God of Prophecy in Luton. In 1995 he established 'Family Matters' as an innovative response to issues of domestic violence in the area. His work has enabled him to establish strategic partnerships with other organisations, including local health practitioners and the local government. The programme is distinctive in that it works not only with the victims, but also with the perpetrators of domestic violence. He is presently pioneering a number of other projects including a Mental Health Advocacy Service for African and Caribbean people in the region. Trevor is aged 40 and married to Paulette. Their daughter, Zena-Marie, is eleven.

Our experience of families is very important. I was born in Guyana in South America, and when I was six months old my parents left me behind to seek out a better life in Britain. My grandmother brought me up until I was seven, when it was decided rather suddenly that I should be sent to join my mother and father in London. It was the first time I'd flown, and I can still remember the plane journey.

Saying goodbye to my grandmother was extremely traumatic, because she was the only parent or security that I'd ever known. (In fact, I would not see her again for more than ten years.) But if leaving my grandmother was difficult, so was adjusting to new family relationships. At first, my mother was very aggressive towards me. And building a relationship with my brother (who I didn't even know existed until I arrived!) was a huge challenge. But before long things were to change again. By the time I was twelve, my parents had divorced and my father moved away from the area. He eventually left the country, and I have rarely seen him since.

As I grew up, I didn't realise how much, and how deeply, these events had affected me. I knew I was hurting, but I presumed that was normal, and tried as hard as I could to ignore it. It wasn't until after I became a Christian in my early twenties that I realised I was unable to bond emotionally with other people. I was extremely fearful of being rejected and so wouldn't allow anyone to get close to me. I began to see that the impact of my parents' divorce had torn me in two. When I tried to read the Bible I couldn't make sense of the concept of the love of God. It talked about God as a father – but what was a father? My idea of a father was someone who walks out on you when you most need him. To the outside world, I was acting as though everything was fine, but I was finally having to face up to the fact that it most definitely wasn't. In one sense, I'd been saved by God, but in another I was totally messed up and broken.

These traumatic family experiences were the foundation on which in 1995 I established the project 'Family Matters'.

A huge part of what happens in our lives is related to our family background. Families really do matter. The goal of Family Matters is to work with those who have had bad experiences of family and particularly with those who have been affected by domestic violence. We help people work through these difficult and emotional issues in order to release them to relate to others in a healthy way. In fact, I describe our vision as 'broken lives restored'.

Family Matters is based in Marsh Farm, which is an estate approximately five miles north of the centre of Luton. Over 10,000 people live there, including a substantial number from African, Caribbean and Asian backgrounds. Marsh Farm has a reputation for being the worst housing estate in the area, and has been the scene of two big riots in recent years. In fact, it has recently won an award of £43 million through the New Deal for Communities initiative, because of the scale of the problems it faces, including high unemployment, housing needs, health and environmental issues, as well as youth delinquency.

I lead a Pentecostal congregation, which is part of the Church of God of Prophecy. It is predominantly an African and Caribbean fellowship, which has been in Luton for about 30 years. However, we only moved onto Marsh Farm in 1990. Our church needed bigger accommodation, and there was a community hall available on the estate, so we took it. The reason is no deeper than that. But, our denomination had been going through a time of national repentance, because we had become too exclusive, and we realised that there was a need for us to have a much greater focus on and involvement in our local communities. So, by the time we moved to Marsh Farm our congregation had become extremely outward-orientated and really wanted to get involved. Our church now has a regular attendance of about 70 adults, but what still surprises everyone is how we are actively involved in our community.

I was asked to become senior pastor of the church in 1997. Prior to moving to the estate, we had lived in an affluent part of Luton. Our neighbours at the time couldn't believe it when we told them of our plans to move. As one person put it, 'People don't sell to move to Marsh Farm; they sell to move away!' However, I felt that the only way to really engage with the community was to be part of it. Much like missionaries who would live in a country in order to be able to understand the culture from the inside, we knew that we needed to be genuinely part of the community – to live out incarnation. Having said all that, I was very nervous about the move, and when the second riot occurred just after we had arrived, my wife and I definitely questioned what we'd done! But we very much sensed that God was leading us onto the estate, and we have found that living here has given us a totally different perception of the area.

As we looked at the community and thought about the cause of the riots, we felt that there was an overwhelming sense of hopelessness and helplessness among the people there. A bit like Nazareth, it was as though people believed that nothing good could come out of Marsh Farm; they were resigned to the fact that they were stuck there and unable to escape its bad reputation. Although the estate has the highest concentration of young people in Luton, there isn't much for them to do and they tend to be frustrated and bored. On top of that, many of them have grown up in family circumstances that do not provide the kind of nurture and encouragement they need. As a result, too many get involved in drugs, crime and other forms of anti-social behaviour. What we saw was that many of those who get involved in these lifestyles believe they're no good and that they'll never amount to anything, because that's all they've ever been told. But without the offer of something concrete to help them see themselves differently and rebuild their lives, they are at real risk of ending up trapped and headed for institutional care.

We wanted to do something to help transform this desperate situation. As a church we own a living message of good news and practical help. Jesus said, 'the Spirit of the Lord is on me, because he has anointed me to preach good news to the poor . . . to proclaim freedom for the prisoners' (Luke 4:18). We knew this must be good news for the people of Marsh Farm. The message of the Christian faith doesn't deny the very real pain of the situation the community faces, yet the power of the resurrection means that no matter what they have been through, there is a future and there is real hope. This is what inspired us – the chance to see individual lives changed, healed and restored in such a way that they could go on to impact other people. When people change, it has the power to transform a community. That's what we believed, but we knew we needed to find a tangible way to demonstrate our faith and effect this personal and social transformation.

We began praying about it and I happened to read in a newspaper about a course in London, which taught basic life skills to give choice to those who had suffered domestic violence. We knew that running a similar course would give our church a method of addressing a big problem on Marsh Farm in a practical way. Domestic violence is a real issue here, which touches many people's lives and includes not just physical and sexual but also huge amounts of emotional and financial abuse. It affects all sorts of people, regardless of age, sex, race or background. And we knew that by teaching life skills, we could give people who felt trapped some way of understanding and dealing with the anger, the stress and the crippling lack of confidence that are so often a cause and result of domestic violence.

So it was that Family Matters was born. We had nine people on our first course, and people haven't stopped coming for help since. We draw on a mixture of pastoral approaches and clinical insights, but the heart of our work is drawn from biblical models of Christian counselling. We advertise our service through local churches and posters, but probably our biggest number of clients come via word of mouth. People who are hurting and who have a lot of unresolved issues in their lives, often find there is nowhere to go for help without feeling stigmatised. Family Matters steps into the void. In fact, we have discovered the course is helpful for everybody and not just those who have experienced domestic violence. On our estate, there is a real hunger for the kind of training we offer. It has had a very broad appeal, and as soon as the word was out that there was no need to feel embarrassed about attending, all sorts of people began to come to us.

Over the years our focus has shifted a little, and at the moment we concentrate on providing one-to-one counselling rather than group courses. Another of our distinctive features is that we work with both the victims and the perpetrators of domestic violence. What surprises some people is that the perpetrators are both men and women. In a typical case, however, a victim might be a woman in her mid-twenties, with one or two children, who is caught in a relationship that has become violent. Such relationships usually start positively, but over time the aggressive partner begins to put the victim down and she starts to lose her confidence. Gradually, he makes her dependent upon him – for example, controlling who she can and cannot see. When they go shopping he determines what she can and cannot have. She finds herself trapped in the relationship, but by this time she has lost all self-confidence and she believes the lies that she is worth nothing. The cycle of violence usually builds up from verbal abuse. The violence may start with slamming doors and smashing things around the house before the full explosion of actual physical assault takes place. Afterwards, it is normal for the perpetrator to express remorse (we call it the 'hearts and flowers' stage because he will say or do anything to win her back) and promise never to do it again. But the cycle will repeat and repeat. The victim becomes trapped because she accepts his promise to be different, and when he's not being violent, she still finds him very pleasant. Her dependence on him has become rooted in her fear of his violence, lack of money and the needs of the children. These factors make it extremely difficult for her to escape the trap she is in.

The first thing we do when such a client comes to see us is to make emergency plans for her protection. We equip her with a list of strategies and telephone contacts in case of trouble. We make her aware of local refuges that are available if she and her children need them. We put her in contact with the local police domestic violence unit, who offer additional safety planning, and ensure that her telephone calls receive priority treatment. We also refer her to her local GP, who is then able to monitor and record any bruises found under examination, which may be the result of domestic violence.

There is no fixed programme for our counselling work with victims. In general, our aim is to build up the victim's confidence and equip them to deal with the problem. One of the first things we do is to affirm their courage in approaching us, because it's a very big step for them to take. We emphasise that they are not responsible for the violence and have not brought it upon themselves. A crucial point for victims to grasp is that there is nothing they can do to change their partners, but that there is plenty they can do to change their circumstances. It is a tough lesson for some of them to learn that by putting up with the violence from their partner they are actually perpetuating it. Ultimately, the victim must take responsibility for gaining control of the situation.

A lot of the work of Family Matters is done through coaching and role-playing to help people develop new patterns of behaviour. For example, I might play the part of the perpetrator and then say, 'If I was behaving this way, how would you deal with it assertively?' In this way, we begin to guide victims towards finding skills and strategies themselves. By the time we've finished the course, a client will have developed the practical ability to seize the initiative. Ultimately this may mean recognising when violence is about to occur and taking evasive action. Or it may involve learning how to defuse the situation before it gets that far. One client went home and said to her partner, 'If you ever touch me again, you will never see me or the kids again.' The simple shock of her standing up for the first time initiated a complete change in that relationship.

It is important to realise that not all victims of domestic violence are women. There are many instances where men are subject to attacks by their female partners. Women can be very strong, and research has shown that they are more likely to use weapons than men (who simply rely on raw brute force). Unfortunately, the idea that men are supposed to be macho and able to cope stops a lot of them from coming forward for assistance.

We also work with the perpetrators of violence. They come on their own initiative, usually because they have reached desperation point. Often the relationship has ended and they have had to face up to the reality of their actions. Initially, many of them come under the guise of some other issue, such as depression. Only once they feel some degree of trust will they open up and admit to their real problem. We recognise that perpetrators need support and help, and that a condemnatory approach will only force them to close up. We never turn them away, but simply build on that initial plea for help and refuse to judge them, however hard that might be.

When a perpetrator talks to us, the first thing we do is to ensure that their family is safe. This is achieved by getting the client's written agreement to ensure the safety of their family during the time that we are working with them, rather than our contacting their family direct. We also contact their GP so that they are aware that their patient is undergoing counselling regarding family issues. A medical examination can be very useful, because it will sometimes reveal that a medical condition is causing the stress and aggression behind the behaviour.

Our primary task is to work with the perpetrators to explore when and how they learnt to use violence as a means of solving a problem. Often, it has been learnt by observing their own violent father or mother during childhood. We give them an assignment where we ask them to keep a record of their emotions, and to particularly describe the feelings they experience and monitor the intensity of them. We then unpack each incident of tension with them. The aim is to work out their standard responses to any given situation and then to teach them new ways of reacting in a non-violent manner. It may sometimes be as simple as going out for a walk when they feel aggressive. We help them to learn to identify the signs that they are getting worked up. For example, they may become aware of their muscles becoming tense, their palms getting sweaty or blood rushing to their head. Again, we re-educate them using role play. In this way new patterns of behaviour are internalised through practice and soon become natural ways of responding. We repeat simulated role plays again and again until the perpetrator has assimilated these new responses. A perpetrator of domestic violence also needs to learn that they cannot change the victim, no matter how much they disagree with them. We teach them that love is about learning to release the other person and respect their freedom to be themselves and make their own choices rather than force them into submission to their will.

At the moment we have a team of seven volunteers. The work is very tough to sustain mentally, emotionally and spiritually, and so we place a great emphasis on supporting each other. I remember counselling a male victim of domestic violence who started to shout and mimic the way his wife threatened and abused him. My colleagues in the next door room thought he was threatening me and got very worried for my safety! We try and make sure that after every counselling session we talk together about the issues that have been raised (without breaking any confidentiality), and then pray for each other. We also receive support through external supervision from a Christian counselling service in Northampton called Manna House.

Our experience of working with people involved in domestic violence has revealed the need for many other issues in the community to be addressed, and so slowly the scope of our work has been growing. For instance, we have now started a parenting skills course, as well as a training course on fatherhood which we run in partnership with another local agency. Recently, we have pioneered a course to work with young people in Luton to broaden their personal development, their interpersonal skills and their sense of confidence and responsibility. Many of these kids will have experienced abuse and violence, and our aim is to break that cycle before it impacts yet another generation.

Another big initiative that we have recently launched is a Mental Health Advocacy Service for the African and Caribbean community in Luton. This project has been commissioned by the Luton Primary Care Trust. Mental health is a massive problem in the UK. In any one year, one in four adults experience some form of mental health problem, and so it has become a government priority to address it. The issue is particularly acute within the African and Caribbean community, where research shows a significant level of discrimination both in terms of misdiagnosis and the withholding of therapies. Mental health advocacy provides a voice for people who are experiencing mental health problems, and enables them to access the services that they are entitled to: for example, if they need access to their medical records, or if they have been sectioned under the Mental Health Act and are being refused access to their family. Because we're looking to restore the dignity of individuals, we have called the project simply 'Dignity'.

Because our work is growing we made the decision to set up and register as a charity, called 'The Family and Relationship Crisis Centre'. Since May 2000 it has provided an umbrella organisation for all we are doing. Our ongoing aim is, of course, to respond even more effectively to the needs that have been identified within the community.

We always charge clients for our work because we believe that it is a way to empower them. It enables them to feel as if they are taking responsibility for themselves and to value the course of action they are taking. For example, a lady who had been subject to domestic violence came to us for help in rebuilding her life after the abusive relationship had ended. One of the forms of abuse she suffered was that she had never been able to go out and spend money or buy clothes for herself. Paying for our services was the first time she had been able to invest in her own life, and it was part of the process of recovery.

However, we only charge according to a person's means, and the fees do not cover our costs, which have to be underpinned in other ways. We receive finances from a number of other sources. For instance, we have been greatly helped by the generous financial (and other practical) support of Tear Fund's Urban Action initiative. Funding has also been made available by a local Anglican church as well as our own. The local council has helped us financially, and we have also received some funding through the Single Regeneration Budget. However, without doubt, the main reason we have been able to survive is because all our counsellors are committed volunteers.

We have tried to develop local partnerships with other groups in the community. The government's New Deal for Communities award has been great at encouraging local welfare organisations to work together. We are developing a good relationship with the local council, and are finding that the historic suspicion they had of Christian 'do-gooders' is fast disappearing. We have also made a point of working with local GPs, and have built up a level of good trust with them. They now recognise our professionalism, and last year we were even asked to conduct a seminar for doctors at Dunstable Hospital on understanding domestic violence issues and the practical steps that GPs can take to help their patients.

It is not always easy, and there have been times over the years when I have felt like giving up. It can be a very lonely walk. When we acquired our building, which acts as our base, I remember looking at all the work that had to be done on it. It lacked any form of central heating and our resources were low. I had given up my job to do this and I had no income whatsoever. Many times I wondered, 'Why am I doing this? There are other things that I could be doing!' Though I have often doubted myself, the truth is that every step of the way God has been faithful. I guess, in the end, I have been sustained by the truth of Scripture passages which keep coming back to me – for instance: 'God will meet all your needs according to his glorious riches in Christ Jesus' (Philippians 4:19).

I don't know if I would have had the strength, determination and encouragement to do this if I wasn't a Christian. I don't think I would have had the vision or drive to say, 'I can make a difference.' Because of my faith, I have a deep sense that this is my purpose for living, and my contribution to society and the community. And so no matter how hard or demanding the work, it has been worthwhile. Personally, I have grown and achieved something I would never have imagined I could. As a church, we have seen God at work and have therefore been greatly enriched. And in terms of the community, fragile lives have been restored and broken relationships healed.

There is still so much to do. But I am confident that God will continue to sustain and bless the work we are doing, and that Marsh Farm is becoming a different place because of it.

Relevant contacts

Care Trust offers a national network of respite care, an advice helpline, and expertise in pregnancy counselling, education, caring, etc.
53 Romney Street
London
SW1P 3RF
Tel: 020 7233 0455
www.care.org.uk

The Children's Society offers a wide range of professional publications which are available online, and are borne out of long experience of working with children.
Edward Rudolf House
69 Margery Street
London WC1X 0JL
Tel: 020 7841 4400
www.the-childrens-society.org.uk

Family Matters publishes a comprehensive guide to resources which can help those working with families.
The Park
Moggerhanger
Bedford MK44 3RW
Tel: 01767 641 002
Email: family@familymatters.org.uk
www.familymatters.org.uk

The Manna House provides counselling and training for counsellors.

St Giles Street

Northampton NN1 1JW

Tel: (01604) 622666 (Bookshop) or 633304 (Counselling)

Email: info@mannahouse.org.uk

Website: www.mannahouse.org.uk

6. Bethany Christian Trust, Edinburgh

Alan Berry founded the Bethany Christian Trust in 1983 in response to the escalating problem of street homelessness in Edinburgh. Over the years he has devised a holistic programme that offers seven levels of care from emergency help and housing through to training programmes that provide all the support necessary for a homeless person to be fully re-integrated into the community. One of the most interesting aspects of the project is the way in which such a large and successful organisation has grown from such a small beginning. The Bethany Christian Trust now employs 79 staff and has an annual budget of nearly £2 million. Alan is married to Anne, and is approaching retirement age.

As a young man I never imagined that I'd become a church minister, and I certainly never thought I'd end up working with the homeless in Scotland. I left school to study at agricultural college, and as a result spent two wonderful years posted in East Africa where, among other things, I had the opportunity to hitchhike to places such as the Victoria Falls and the Kariba Dam. During this time, I decided that I wanted to use my skills long term overseas, serving as a missionary. So I went off to train at London Bible College, after which my wife and I planned to move to Peru.

It was only when our dream fell through that we returned to my native Glasgow, and someone suggested I should think about becoming a local minister. Within four months I found myself pastoring a Baptist church in Fife. We had a good time there, and nine happy years later I was approached by another Baptist church, at South Leith in Edinburgh, to become their minister. It was while working there that I first came into contact with the problem of homelessness, and the vision for Bethany Christian Trust was birthed.

Leith sits to the north-east of Edinburgh city centre on the road that runs down the hill towards the docks. The area itself is both residential and industrial. In recent years there has been some significant redevelopment, and the funnels of the Royal Yacht Britannia have become a local landmark on the skyline. The people are hard-working and there is a strong community spirit, but the area also has many social problems.

At South Leith I became increasingly aware of people arriving at the church door who were homeless. Ministers are, of course, often visited by people dropping by for some supper or a cup of soup, but as the years went by, and particularly in the early 1980s, the trickle was becoming a torrent. There have always been tramps around, people who choose a homeless lifestyle. But this was different. These people were driven on to the streets by virtue of their circumstances – they had no other option. Some were battling with addictions such as alcohol or drugs; others had fallen into crime or suffered family breakdown or mental illness. This led them to lose their tenancy or home, and forced them into sleeping rough. Homelessness is a huge problem across Edinburgh, not just in Leith. In fact, it is estimated by SHELTER and the City Council that about 10,000 people are made homeless here in any one year.

At the same time as recognising this surge in homelessness, I found myself drawn to preaching on some of Jesus' words, such as 'love your neighbour' and 'in as much as you have done it unto one of these the least of my brothers you have done it unto me'. Then, standing at the church door afterwards, I would again be confronted by someone else who had nowhere to sleep that night. It was obvious that, as a church, we were espousing a message of hope and salvation that we were not living out in practice.

In 1981, while I was still grappling with this issue, a building opposite our church came on to the property market. My first thought was that we should buy it and set up a work for homeless people. Circumstances proved it to be the wrong timing and the property was sold to someone else. But it was as if God had given me a vision for the future, and a couple of years later my wife and I met two other friends to begin to talk seriously about making it happen. As a result, the four of us decided to form the Bethany Christian Trust, which was set up with full charitable status in 1983. Our goal was to provide accommodation for homeless people in a hostel. But we also wanted to address the underlying causes of their homelessness, and liaise on their behalf with the authorities where appropriate. For us, the name Bethany Christian Trust is very significant. Bethany was an important place in Jesus' ministry. It was a place where he stayed, where he had friends, where he enjoyed good food and company, where he experienced joy and sadness, and where he gave back life and promised a future – not only in time but for eternity. We call it Bethany 'Christian' Trust, because we want it to be recognised that Christian faith is at the core of all we have to offer. Our key aim is to demonstrate Christ's love for homeless and vulnerable people.

We needed to find a suitable property to start the hostel, and so we began to look around. This was a huge task, because we only had a small budget and because we had to face the 'Not In My Back Yard' syndrome. Local people were very ready to applaud the kind of work we wanted to do, as long as it wasn't on their street! However, it was just at this time that we discovered the original property opposite the church was back on the market! Unfortunately the price had more than doubled, but the amazing thing was that the owner had managed to obtain a 'House of Multiple Occupancy' licence, because she had wanted to set up a commercial hotel. This meant that we wouldn't need to apply for planning permission, and so we could start without protracted negotiations with local residents.

At the time, interest rates were around 16 per cent, and we couldn't get a bank to fund us. We eventually found a firm in Torquay to lend us the money at a cheaper rate because they wanted to invest in good causes. Even so, it took us a long time to pay off that first loan. But we were in business at long last! The first residents moved in to the Bethany Christian Centre on the 4th April 1983.

However, it didn't take us long to realise that our

property was really too small for what we ideally wanted to achieve. So I suggested to the trustees that we purchase the adjacent derelict building in order to extend the centre and to create a manager's flat. When they agreed, I naïvely asked the church for three months' leave of absence in order to do the conversion work myself. The job was vastly bigger and more complex than I'd realised, and the best part of a year later I was still working on it and getting nowhere. It nearly killed me. I regularly felt as though I was in a tunnel and could hardly see a pin of light at the end. It was one of the most difficult times I've ever known.

We couldn't afford outside contractors, and so the only help I could get was from volunteers. They were very enthusiastic, but could be very hard to manage. Some of them were unteachable – they knew how the job should be done much better than me or anyone else, and weren't ready to listen to anyone who disagreed! But there were many times when, after they all went home, I would have to undo their work and spend hours preparing for them to come back the next day. A bit like Laurel and Hardy, I wondered: 'How did I get myself into this mess?' I wanted to finish the job, but felt that I was running out of the emotional or physical strength I needed to do it. I was still the minister of the church and responsible for preaching and undertaking all the emergency visiting, as well as working my fingers to the bone on the extension. And my task was made even harder by loads of people who told me they thought I was crazy, was clearly burning myself out and wasn't doing the right thing.

I have to say that it was only God who kept me going. And his provision was to become very clear one day when an elderly retired joiner wandered in to help me. He was a skilled craftsman, and I think it must have frustrated him trying to work with the rest of us 'handymen', because one day he set down his parameters by announcing, 'Just leave all this end of the building to me.' However, when his son (an architect) heard about this he was very concerned, as his father was in his seventies. Though the old man had the ability, his son feared he didn't have the strength to do the work. So he came to visit me, and standing in the midst of what was a bomb site, looked me in the eye and said, 'How would you like it if, at no cost to you, I brought in some professionals to finish this end?' It seemed too good to be true! Within a week he had three qualified tradesmen in, as well as an apprentice, with the order, 'Do whatever Mr Berry asks you to.' They worked constantly for nine or ten weeks. The progress was incredible. When they had finished, the son came back to see me and said we didn't have to pay for anything other than the paint. Tragically, he died shortly afterwards, but I will always remember him and his work as an absolute Godsend for Bethany Christian Trust.

Over the course of the next year I had to think carefully about my own role. I was trying to manage Bethany from a distance, as well as continuing as a full-time minister. I knew that I had to make a choice. Should I remain as pastor of South Leith Baptist and stay hands-off with the trust? Or should I take the step of going full time? To do so would be a major risk, because at that stage the trust had a massive debt and no resources. I sought some advice from a few people I really trusted. One of them said, 'Alan, your eyes light up whenever you talk about Bethany. There is something in it that God has given to you.' As I was driving home and thinking about what had been said to me, I saw a huge roadside advertising poster with the words 'Go For It' displayed. I still don't know what it was advertising, but the truth is that it hit me like a blinding light. There was no longer any doubt. I resigned from the church and joined Bethany full time as manager. That was in late 1984.

Anne and I moved into the hostel and spent the next six years looking after the 26 residents. However, as the staff team grew in terms of expertise and numbers, I was able to concentrate on developing other areas of the work. A key step was the fostering of our relationship with the housing and social work departments of the council. In 1991 we were eventually formally registered to work with people with special needs: those with mental health issues and addictions. It was this point that marked the transitional step as we moved away from simply being perceived as Christian 'do gooders' to becoming a professional service. And the funding that ensued from rent and care allowances meant that we could enjoy our first period of financial stability, which enabled us to grow. From this stable platform, we were able to purchase three flats to set up our 'supported accommodation' department, which is able to offer continuing back-up to those people who have left our centre as part of their reintegration into the community.

It is amazing to look back and see just how far Bethany Christian Trust has grown. From the acquisition of our first property in 1983 at a cost of £44,000, the trust now has a property portfolio of about £2.5 million. From one member of staff we now have a team of nearly 100, including 20 full-time volunteers. The salary of our only employee cost £720 in 1983. This year it looks as though the budget will include £1.1 million for salaries alone! The total budget in 1983 was just a few thousand pounds, whereas today it is £1.75 million per annum.

We visualise Bethany's work in terms of seven progressive levels of care. Our aim is to provide a continuum of care from emergency help on the streets through to total reintegration into the community. Our goal is to empower homeless people to achieve their potential. We often explain that 'opportunity knocks' at every level of the work we do, because each offers our clients the opportunity to grasp change.

I describe the first four levels of care as the 'ladder' out of the pit of homelessness. The first rung is our emergency street work. This centres around our Care Van, which acts as a port of call for those sleeping rough in the city. It provides soup, rolls and blankets, together with friendship and advice every night of the year, and is completely staffed by voluntary teams. In winter, when temperatures can get dangerously low, we also run a night shelter for rough sleepers. The project is largely staffed by volunteers and uses church venues across the city on a rota basis. This year the council gave us £33,000 as provision for three night care workers. Both these emergency schemes are run in partnership with Edinburgh City Mission and local churches.

The second rung of our ladder is emergency accommodation for those that are ready to move off the streets. In 1993 we purchased an old tea factory, and converted it into a short-term resettlement unit called Bethany House. It accommodates up to 28 homeless men and women for a period of three months at a time. It is staffed 24 hours a day. The emphasis is on helping people to move into more secure housing elsewhere, and to develop the practical living skills such as cooking, budgeting and personal hygiene that they will need in order to survive. A big emphasis in our work is on changing people's view of themselves, as so many of them suffer from low self-esteem and insecurity. Our aim here is to sensitively help our clients to set goals for their lives and then to work out how to achieve them successfully.

The third rung of our ladder offers more structured specialist resettlement over a longer period of time. The Bethany Christian Centre, which we originally bought across the road from South Leith Baptist Church, is now used as a Welfare-to-Work hostel. It houses 16 men in a community setting, and uses an individually tailored programme of care and training to move people off benefits and into work, at the same time equipping them for life back in the community. Residents will stay with us for six months to a year. Recent statistics show that 81 per cent of those who left this unit last year are now in their own tenancies or homes, and 66 per cent of them are in some form of voluntary or paid work or training. We also now have a farm, west of the city, where we hope to develop a community environment in which to offer agricultural training and advice in a Christian context.

Fourthly, we offer 'supported' medium and long-term furnished tenancies in the community. Each resident has a support worker who provides a level of help to meet their needs without encouraging a dependency syndrome. This represents the final step out of homelessness, because it reintroduces people into independent living. We presently have 51 supported flats with accommodation for 68 people. Normally, people will start in a shared tenancy before eventually moving into a tenancy of their own. Each has a responsibility to cook, budget, clean and look after their own home. We have set up a befriending scheme to link tenants with people from local churches who help in creating new, healthy social networks to replace the unhelpful influences many of our residents have left behind.

Our final three levels of care integrate with and work alongside our first four rungs. So, fifthly, we have developed a service for those facing alcohol or drug addiction. Up to 80 per cent of those coming to stay in trust accommodation have a history of abuse of alcohol or drugs. The Bethany Addiction Team offers advice and help to those on each rung of the trust's work. It works with clients to teach new ways of coping with life's pressures. Although, it has to be said, this is a long and difficult process, we have the privilege of seeing many people break free of their addictions.

Sixthly, we have set up a homemaking service. Bethany Homemaker helps turn houses into homes. Our aim is to provide home furnishings help to people who have successfully come off the streets to get themselves established and feel 'at home' in their new accommodation. It is common for people to move into a tenancy that is completely unfurnished, but find themselves with no ability to pay for essential pieces of furniture such as a cooker or a bed. By offering such items at nominal cost we provide a very practical way of helping, not only those who have been homeless, but also other people in the community who find it hard to afford basic home furnishings. The project works on a referral basis. When a client has been referred to us, we fill out an application form for them and then work at getting funding for them through grant-making trusts and organisations. Once we have a positive response we invite the client back and they are able to choose what they want according to the budget they have received. For instance, we have a very good link with the local John Lewis department store. When they deliver a new cooker to a customer, they recover the old one and then pass it on to us. We have an electrician who reconditions it before we sell it at a nominal price, with a guarantee and the costs of installation included. We have been able to furnish whole flats for as little as £300. And we sell new carpet from as little as £3 a square metre! As part of this aspect of Bethany Homemaker, we now also run six charity shops, which, besides selling good furniture cheaply, create some income for us and also provide some of our residents with an ideal work experience opportunity, as well as giving us a 'shop window' on to the community.

Our seventh and final level of care is training. If meeting the immediate housing needs of homeless people is important, so too is empowering them for a meaningful life of future employment. Almost without exception, those who come to Bethany are unemployed. Many are unable to read and do not have the confidence or ability to access the information they need to make informed choices about their lives. So we run Adult Basic Education courses on reading, writing and arithmetic. We also teach life skills, job seeking skills and a basic IT course. We have been able to develop a good working relationship with a local college, which accredits some of our courses, and have been pleased that a number of our students have even progressed on to further courses there through distance learning. We also provide our clients with tutorial support where necessary.

We run a drop-in clinic on Tuesday mornings that tends to act as a hub for the rest of the training work we do. We run classes to develop skills in creative writing, art and drama and provide work placements and voluntary work experience opportunities. Our aim is to move progressively from providing the basic life skills necessary for independent living through to specific pre-vocational training that equips people to find and succeed in a job that suits them.

We believe that it is tremendously important that our faith stays at the heart of Bethany Christian Trust. Our whole ethos is to provide a holistic response to the needs of homeless people in the name of Jesus Christ. We are a Christian organisation giving a professional service. People often ask which is the more important: that we feed people's bodies or that we save their souls? The truth is I don't believe that such a question is legitimate. When Jesus was confronted with hungry people he fed them, and when there were sick people he healed them. But he also constantly taught his message. It was all interwoven into who he was. You couldn't separate out the strand. The verses I most often preach on when I am asked to speak about the trust are from Isaiah 61, as quoted in the Nazareth Manifesto. Jesus said he came 'to preach good news to the poor . . . to bind up the broken hearted, to proclaim freedom for the captives and release from darkness for the prisoners.' In Jesus' ministry, physical well-being and spiritual release are all bound up together. So at Bethany, we aim to provide a holistic response that ministers to the whole person with the whole gospel.

We have seen lots of people become Christians through the work of Bethany. All our staff and volunteers are Christians, and there are many opportunities for them to share their faith. In our key-work sessions we address all the needs of the person and quite properly this includes asking a person how they feel about the spiritual aspect of their life. We have daily prayers that are open to all our residents, and grace is said before each meal. The staff are welcome to invite people to church, providing there is no pressure, and there are plenty of other opportunities to talk about faith, such as over coffee in the evenings. We also run a full-time discipleship course for a small group of people in the old manager's flat adjacent to the centre, which has been incredibly successful. But it is vital to stress that all of these are quite voluntary activities. There is never any spiritual pressure on any of our clients to fit in, in any way. Our Christian emphasis is never forced on people, and everybody gets exactly the same service whether they are interested in Christ or not.

However, one of the things that has become evident over the years is that non-verbal communication is the most effective way of ministering the love of Christ. The homeless people in our care often express how the love that is shown by the staff team has provoked their interest. We believe that we have to earn the right to share the gospel.

We do not believe in buttonholing people. Once, someone accused us of brainwashing, and the Director of Social Work for the city was obliged to instigate a full investigation. Afterwards, he went to press and said, 'I have had this matter fully investigated, and I found absolutely no grounds to say that Bethany was brainwashing.' That was about five years ago, and we haven't had any such accusation since.

Having said all this, I do not believe we should apologise for our commitment to the gospel at Bethany. About two-thirds of our income comes through public funding, such as housing benefit, care allowance, money for New Deal placements, grants for particular forms of training and so on. My view is that I do not think the local council ought to pay us for evangelism, and I don't think it would be fair for us to ask them to do so. However, the other third of our income comes from Christian sources, including individuals, churches and grant-making trusts. So we could legitimately say that one-third of our time could be used in evangelism.

We have two categories of volunteers who work for us. First, there are those who come to give a year of their time, such as young people who have just finished at university. Second, we are training some of the homeless people who come through our hostels and discipleship house, which is a way of giving them some great work experience for the future. In fact, a significant number of our staff have themselves been helped out of homelessness through the work of the trust. For example, one of our current assistant managers was hospitalised in an acute psychiatric ward in the summer of 1996 for alcoholism and drug abuse. He had been living on the streets for about two years, and the doctor said he was well on the way to killing himself. He detoxed for two weeks before coming to Bethany, where he joined the short-term resettlement unit, and then spent six months rehabilitating in the centre. Here he experienced a life-changing encounter with Christ and God's mercy. His life was transformed. Today he is free of his addictions, and has now been married for three years. Though he started working with us as a volunteer, he is now one of our full-time salaried deputy managers and is doing a very good job for us.

We have developed relationships with a number of other organisations. I have mentioned the Social Work Department, the Edinburgh City Mission and the local college. But we also work with other mental health and homeless agencies, and refer people to such organisations according to the specialist expertise they need. We have also worked hard at building good working relationships with the churches across Edinburgh – because in the end we see ourselves simply as an extension of their work. It is as though we are the church's arms and legs out in the community doing the work that is too specialised for it to be able to do on its own. Some churches offer us prayer support and others give financially. Some provide volunteers and some help us with the emergency night shelter. We enjoy a great deal of practical support and backing, from them, which we greatly appreciate.

The most amazing thing has been to see the way that the project has grown from such a small beginning. As I look back, it is a privilege to see the way in which God has brought us success in so many different ways. In a materialistic world it would be easy to get excited by the increase in turnover or in the property portfolio. But the really exciting thing is the change in people. We have seen those who are hungry on the street being fed. We have seen hundreds of people desperate to get off the street finding resettlement in and through Bethany House. We have seen many with addictions to drugs or gambling or pornography overcoming them. We have witnessed people gaining the confidence and qualifications to get a job, and then going on to fulfil their potential back in the community. And we continue to see people coming into a relationship with the Lord. It has been a tremendous privilege to be involved in such work. But our last annual report was entitled 'Much Accomplished. . . So Much More To Do'. If we want to continue making a real dent in the number of concrete pillows used every night around the city, then much still requires to be done. I might be approaching retirement age now, but my vision for Bethany Christian Trust has a long way to go!

Relevant contacts

Adullam Homes Housing Association
The Old Courthouse
11/13 New Road
Lymm
Cheshire WA13 9DX
Tel: 01925 752100
Email: info@adullam.org.uk
Web: www.adullam.org.uk

Churches National Housing Coalition
Central Buildings
Oldham Street
Manchester M1 1JT
Tel: 0161 236 9321
Email: coalition@justhousing.co.uk

CRASH and the Joseph Rowntree Foundation have produced a comprehensive guide to single homelessness, which is free to voluntary agencies. For a copy, call 020 8742 0717 or email crash@clara.net

Edinburgh City Mission
9 Pilrig Street
Edinburgh EH6 5AH
Tel: 0131 554 6140
Email: post@ecm.org.uk
www.ecm.org.uk

Habitat for Humanity Great Britain creates innovative, practical solutions to housing needs which draw communities together.
11 Parsons Street
Banbury
Oxon OX16 5LW
Tel: 01295 264 240
Email: mkearney@hfhgb.org
www.hfhgb.org

For a starter pack guide to working with the homeless, call the **Scottish Churches Housing Agency** on 0131 477 4556 or email diane@scotchho.org.uk

For a comprehensive directory of agencies that work with homeless people, see www.homelesspages.org.uk

7. Cornerstone Community Project, Swansea

Julian Richards and his wife, Sarah, established the Cornerstone Church in Swansea in 1990. Their vision is for a church which impacts its community through evangelistic actions as well as words. Cornerstone runs a number of different initiatives in such areas as children's work, counselling and family support. One of the most exciting schemes is an innovative project called 'The Gap', which is a development programme for disaffected youth. The Gap has seen remarkable success, has won a number of national awards and been an inspiration to teachers up and down the country. Julian is aged 39. He and Sarah have three children.

I was a very disillusioned young man at the age of 16. I had dropped out of school (at the suggestion of the staff, who felt I was making no effort there!), and was making a bit of money singing protest songs in Cardiff night clubs. But it wasn't so much that I was disillusioned with school itself as that I was generally disillusioned with the whole world. I was very aware of global problems, like the arms race, poverty and suffering, and it all seemed so over-whelming. It seemed to me that for all our education we hadn't developed much as a society. So I decided to drop out and search for an alternative lifestyle that would make a real difference.

I was a convinced atheist because I couldn't see any evidence of God in the environment around me. I didn't come from a Christian background, but one day, at the age of 19, I was walking through the woods at Castle Coch, and out of the blue I heard God speak to me. It wasn't an audible voice, but somehow deep in my spirit, and with words that I could clearly understand, God said, 'Abandon yourself to me, proclaim my name to all people and I will meet all your needs!' Suddenly I was aware of God's presence all around me, and I sensed his power in creation. It was utterly awesome, like an explosion. I had a deep conviction of my sin, and I knew that I had to make a decision. I chose there and then to follow God and his call upon my life. I realised I needed to get to know the personality behind this great power, and I had a thought that I should start reading the Bible. I felt that this idea was from God, and so took up feverishly reading the Bible every single night for about three months. As I did, I grew to understand more about Jesus and I began to pray and develop a relationship with him. All I can say is that it was an extraordinary and extremely exciting time.

Before long I joined a local Pentecostal church. I was on the dole at the time, and I began to travel around with an evangelist, who was based there working in schools and on the streets. It was while I was working with him in Bath that I first met Sarah, who was later to become my wife. At the age of 22 we enrolled to study at Bible College, and it was there that we became convinced of the importance of the role of the local congregation in the community. We got the sense that God was calling us to invest our lives in the local church and to assist and help equip it to function more effectively in society. So when, after finishing college, Sarah and I were invited to work as youth pastors in a church in Hereford, we seized the opportunity with both hands. That was in 1986.

It was during this time that I was invited to do some teaching for a group of churches in Wales on the subject of the church and community evangelism. I decided to explore the topic from scratch and take a fresh look at the issues for myself. It was as I studied the Bible again that it dawned on me that there are two sides of the coin called 'evangelism': preaching and serving – or, put another way, words and works. It seemed to me that while evangelical churches are generally very good at using words to express their message, they are often far weaker when it comes to providing physical models of service in the community. Most of our faith is expressed within the four walls of our church buildings. However, I felt that effective evangelism needed to pay equal regard to both sides of the coin once again. I could see that when this doesn't happen, people are at risk of rejecting Christianity, not because of the image or message of Jesus Christ, but because of the carica-ture of the church. Jesus' words, 'Let your light shine before men that they may see your good deeds and praise your Father in heaven' have become very important to me.

Sarah and I were in Hereford for three years, and then in 1990 felt a very clear sense that we should move to

Swansea. God miraculously provided us with a house beyond our normal means, and so we started to pray that he would reveal what he wanted us to do. Around this time, we went to a conference in Prestatyn on the theme of church planting and pioneering. It was while we were there that we had a deep sense that the reason God had brought us to Swansea was to plant a new church in order to find ways of communicating the gospel to a local community, both through preaching and Christ-like service.

So it was that in 1990 we started the Cornerstone Church in the Penderry ward to the north of Swansea. Penderry is one of the most deprived wards in Wales, which, in turn, is one of the poorest countries in Western Europe. The estate we work on has 12,000 houses on it. It suffers from all the typical problems of large social housing estates, such as drug abuse, car crime, high unemployment (especially among the youth) and a high teenage pregnancy rate.

Because we had already seen a number of people become Christians since arriving in Swansea, we were able to start the church in our house with nine members. In fact, I remember that our first offering was £35! Right from the beginning we started with a vision and commitment to serve the local community. So we developed a link with the local school to run kids clubs and help some of the children with their reading. We started running a youth club in the local community centre. And another idea was that whenever the community put on a 'fun day' we would make sure we were part of it. Gradually we were able to establish trust with the community, and slowly we built a reputation as a church that wanted to serve local people.

As the church started to grow I realised that we needed to find new accommodation. We moved to a school hall, but I still remember the day when I drove past the local GPO sorting office and was surprised to see that it was up for sale. I knew the building well and had always thought that it would be an ideal place for a church centre. It seemed an ideal environment from which we could develop strategic projects and expand our work in the community. So I made enquiries and discovered that the asking price was £34,500. The income levels of our congregation are reflective of the economic environment in which we live, and there are no professionals such as lawyers or doctors in the church. So the idea of buying, refurbishing, resourcing and staffing such a centre presented a significant challenge. But still we felt that it was the right thing to do if our work was to continue growing rather than to stagnate.

As a church we managed to raise £8,000 for the deposit and get a mortgage for the rest. However, buying the building was one thing; the real challenge was refurbishing it. We wanted to develop it to incorporate facilities, including counselling rooms, a fitness and health area, an IT suite and space for youth activities. I remember praying, 'Lord, we don't have enough resources to do what you have called us to do; we don't have the people to do what you have called us to do; we don't have the finances to do what you have called us to do. You have to provide what we need in order to move this thing forward. You are our only hope.' I felt the Lord clearly answer me and say, 'As you need it I will provide it.'

Within a week a friend from Hereford, who knew

nothing about our situation, phoned me and said, 'I was praying the other day and I felt that God wants me to move to Swansea to work with you.' He is particularly skilled at project development, and became a tremendous asset to us. For instance, one of the things he did was to bring in our first batch of funding of £15,000 towards the cost of refurbishment. Through quite considerable sacrifice the congregation managed to collect another £15,000. But we were still massively short and I had no idea where we would find the rest of the finance we needed. However, a couple of weeks later, I was preaching at another local church where, out of the blue, a businessman came up to me because he had heard about our new building. He asked if he could come and see it and, after having looked round it, explained that he was in the refurbishment trade and wanted to do all the work we needed for the money we had raised so far. The work he agreed to carry out was priced at about £90,000, but he did an absolutely top quality professional job for £30,000! At around the same time, we received a grant from a non-Christian trust who were so impressed with what we were doing that they offered to fund a development officer to work with us for the next three years. So God answered our prayers in a very powerful way.

Though we bought the building in 1994, it was a further three years before it was finally commissioned for use on the 28th February 1997. We made good use of the intervening period to train our staff and volunteers in preparation for the task ahead. We trained people in all sorts of skills, from National Vocational Qualifications in specialised areas such as aerobics to advanced counselling courses and local authority youth work. We also continued building relationships and developing projects in the community, which we could later expand in the centre. By the time it opened, because the local people knew and trusted us, they were inclined to use our services and facilities. I'm still convinced that things would have worked out very differently if we had tried to just come in and parachute services on them without any previous relationship.

One of the most successful projects we run is called 'The Gap', which grew out of a vision to meet the needs of the community's disaffected young people. Twenty per cent of the youngsters in our local schools are struggling academically. Many of those we work with come from troubled backgrounds where, for instance, they may have been involved in crime and have got themselves in some sort of trouble with the police. Some have been thrown out of their homes. A lot have experienced drug or alcohol abuse. Nearly all of them have low and irregular school attendance. Some of the kids are into car crime and in one year 5 out of 15 girls on The Gap were pregnant, and all of them were aged under 16.

Every one of these kids has potential, but all they have ever known is failure at school. So we developed The Gap to provide an alternative educational curriculum. It is more than just a youth project for helping troubled kids; it's a whole new system that re-educates, re-motivates and re-engages youngsters who have been alienated by traditional forms of education and learning. The problem with the normal model of learning is that it just doesn't suit everyone. There is obviously a deep need for new models of education that release the potential of young people who are demotivated and disempowered by conventional techniques.

Our primary programme is offered to a local girls' school. Each year we take 15 girls in their final year of school and work with them every Tuesday, Wednesday and Thursday from September through to April. (We also run similar schemes with other schools over the summer period.) The kids we work with are usually the toughest and most disruptive in the school. The teachers send them to us simply because they are so difficult for them to handle. We take them through training for qualifications from the Open College Network, then on Mondays and Fridays they go back to school to take GCSEs in Maths, English and Science, as well as getting involved in community projects.

There are a number of distinctive aspects to our approach. First, we work with the same group throughout the whole course. This creates a strong sense of community, which is something that too often these youngsters don't receive elsewhere. It also helps to provide some of the security and consistency they need in order to concentrate and give themselves more fully to the learning process. Learning is always difficult for people who are disturbed, emotionally insecure or malnourished.

Second, we emphasise essential life skills, rather than traditional academic subjects. So we teach about issues like relationships, communication, expectations, community awareness, handling emotions, job interviews and money, which help them to cope with and negotiate life once they leave school. Without these skills they are at huge risk of getting pregnant, becoming unemployed and getting involved in some form of crime.

Third, we use creative models in order to hold their interest. Because many of these kids have very low attention spans, we are drawing on our 15 years of experience in connecting with youth in church settings, and simply applying the same principles to an educational programme. For example, we ensure a wide mix of interesting topics, and work hard at giving early response and feedback. Each course is started and examined within a fortnight, and so there is no need for the students to wait until the end of the year to find out whether or not they passed. This has the effect of keeping their motivation up, because once they find they can succeed, they get the taste for it and it encourages them to go for more. It is evident they enjoy themselves from the massive increase in attendance rates. Often we have seen these improve from as little as 20 per cent to over 90 per cent. At the same time, their grades improve substantially, and many end up leaving us not only with life-skill qualifications from The Gap, but also with success in their GCSEs back at school. Without The Gap they would definitely have left school with no qualifications and no prospects. As it is, we have seen as many as 11 of the 15 children in a year group go on to higher education or employment. Believe me, that is quite an astonishing turnaround.

Poverty has a big effect on young people's attitudes, morality and spirituality. Where there is poverty there is usually poor education, lack of opportunity and a resulting lack of hope. This in turn leads to a downward spiral. One of the reasons why so many of the young girls become pregnant is because they don't see themselves as having any real choices for the future. For instance, they don't have to think about whether or not it will mess up their chance of going to college or university. When you don't feel you have any choices you don't have to be careful. So poverty, hopelessness, teenage delinquency and pregnancy are all connected. The Gap is significant because it re-empowers the participants with choice. There is a high motivation for these kids to come to The Gap, because they see it as a real opportunity to change their lives and get a better future. The greatest thing on offer for them at The Gap is hope.

As the course progresses, we witness a clearly detectable shift in the students' attitudes. Both teachers and parents often comment on this change. They become much more communicative and happy. Instead of going home stroppy and disappearing into their rooms to play their music, they have something to share about their day. People in the community have commented on how there is less trouble on the streets now, and even how the youngsters are help-ing to carry older people's shopping off the bus and back home for them! I remember one girl who was continually getting arrested and first came to The Gap accompanied by a police liaison officer. By the end of the course she wanted to work in the police force herself and went off to college to get the necessary qualifications!

We have faced surprisingly few discipline problems. This is partly because we get the pupils to agree their own contract at the beginning of the course, which therefore they have obligations to keep to. Second, we withdraw all the unnecessary institutional boundaries – such as having to wear school uniform. Our timetable is also much more flexible than usual and varies from day to day, depending not only on the subject but our pupils' attention span.

A very important principle for us is that because The Gap is an educational programme, we respect the trust of the schools and parents, and never manipulate the situation in order to evangelise. However, if we are asked why we do what we do, then we will always answer the question. We've seen some young people become Christians and others hopefully will in the future. But quite besides that, if their experience of Cornerstone has helped to break down their suspicion of the church, then that is a very positive influence in their lives.

We have a great team who run The Gap. Sarah, my wife, is a qualified teacher. She directs the project and writes the courses. We also have an outward-bound instructor and three youth workers. A real boost was when we won the Welsh Agency Youth Award for being one of the most effective projects in Wales, which was presented to us by the first Secretary of Wales from the Welsh Assembly. We have also been asked to speak at numerous headmasters' conferences on Youth Disaffection, because The Gap is one of the few models across the country that really does tackle the problems effectively.

Cornerstone also runs a counselling service. Some of the members of our church have trained to an advanced level in counselling, and as a result we have subsequently been able to develop a partnership with a local medical centre. We are effectively the GPs of the counselling world for our local community. If somebody goes to their doctor with a relevant problem, the doctor will then refer them on to us.

They phone us and we fix an appointment with the counsellor who we think is most appropriate. Examples of the sort of situation we might help with include relationship issues, redundancy or depression. In situations of grief counselling we offer a maximum of six one-hour sessions to support clients through the emotional time of crisis. If the situation requires longer-term or more specialist help then we refer them to a more appropriate agency. The counselling we offer is not expressly Christian, although we always give clients the opportunity to address spiritual factors if they so wish.

Other projects Cornerstone runs include 'Little Rascals', which is a programme designed to help equip mothers about how to relate to their pre-school kids more effectively and how to communicate and play with them educationally in order to put the right foundations in place for when they get to school. We also offer preparatory help for marriage and parenting, and run courses on dealing with relationships and resolving conflict. On top of this we have a computer suite where we run courses in IT training, such as word processing and spreadsheets. We also have a youth club on Fridays. We used to run fitness and aerobics classes until the local health centre started running similar courses and there was no longer any need.

Cornerstone is also involved in pioneering 'Gweini' (Welsh for 'to serve'), which is a joint project developed with the Evangelical Alliance in Wales, Care for Wales and Tearfund. Our task is to represent churches that are engaged in community work to the Welsh Assembly and to support, advise and assist them as they develop good practice. We also help to make them aware of funding issues and the changes in social work and legislation, which impact their work.

Cornerstone Church now has a congregation of around 100 people, including children. Nearly all of them live in the local community. We have had to work very hard on our pastoral structures. Almost all the volunteers and staff for the community project are from the congregation, so finding the right balance between pastoring them and releasing them to serve the community is very important. The leadership team has a responsibility to continually monitor and assess where the church is at and to make sure that people are neither buckling under the burden of the work, nor settling into too much comfort. It is a delicate balance. It is important that no single project demands too much of the church's resources or becomes the all-consuming vision within the church.

It hasn't always been easy. When you're pioneering from scratch there is a lot of sacrifice involved. It can be tiring and very hard work. There have been times of immense challenges of faith and perseverance for us all. Funding is also an ongoing issue – our budget is over £100,000 per year. We have been given financial support by a number of trusts, but finance is always a challenge. However, God has always been faithful and provided. We wouldn't really have been able to do anything that we've managed to achieve over the years if we were solely dependent upon the means of our congregation. We have slowly learnt that as we have been faithful in releasing the resources and energies we do have on behalf of the poor, God has poured out his blessing to meet our needs. Our experience suggests that God really does have a heart for a church that brings practical hope into the community, and I am confident that as we continue to be obedient to our calling he will continue to prosper our work.

Relevant contacts

Church Pastoral Aid Society provides a range of resources, publications and projects for working with children and young people.
Athena Drive
Tachbrook Park
Warwick CV34 6NG
Tel: 01926 458 458
Email: info@cpas.org.uk
www.cpas.org.uk

GWEINI A partnership of the Evangelical Alliance Wales, CARE for Wales, Cornerstone Church and Tearfund Wales, which equips and networks churches engaged in faith-based welfare through conferences and other resources.
PO Box 601
Cardiff CF10 1YR
Tel: (029) 2023 2852
Email: info@gweini.org.uk

Ichthus Community Projects encompass a wide range of successful programmes, including work with schools/ education and young people (XLP), unemployment, credit unions and addiction.

The Georgian House
31 East Dulwich Grove
London SE22 8PH
Tel: 020 8299 5500
Email: admin@ichthus.org

Positive Parenting provide resources and training materials with the aim of developing parenting skills, supporting families and working with people who have learning disabilities.

2A South Street
Gosport PO12 1ES
Tel: 023 9252 8787
Email: Info@parenting.org.uk
www.parenting.org.uk

8. City Gateway, London

Dirk Paterson is the co-founder and chair of City Gateway in Spitalfields, East London. City Gateway was established in September 1999 to provide IT training, together with employment preparation and work placements, for the long-term unemployed in Tower Hamlets. Dirk's motivation is to break through the 'glass wall' that separates those living in real poverty in Spitalfields from the growing prosperity and affluence of the City of London 500 yards away. He is aged 29 and he fits his work with City Gateway around his full-time job as a parliamentary lobbyist for the London Chamber of Commerce.

Being unemployed was one of the worst experiences of my life. Up to that point I had been very successful. I had a good degree and was awarded a number of undergraduate prizes, and had just finished working as an intern in Parliament where I was writing speeches for an MP. But then I couldn't find a job and found myself scratching a living together cleaning floors and giving the odd music lesson. I ended up as a runner, making cups of coffee for a

TV company! It was grim. They treated me badly and paid me late. I remember the climax of this rather depressing period when I had to plug little holes in the office floor where rats had been getting through. I felt so down on myself. Was this all I was capable of? Was this all I was worth? The feeling of low self-esteem was so acute and debilitating that I didn't even want to get up in the morning. I felt that I had absolutely nothing to contribute to the world. The feeling is still very clear in my memory. In fact, I hope it always will be, because it has been highly motivating in that it has given me a real compassion for all those who have no work. It has enabled me to understand how being gainfully employed is so important for the human soul. This understanding was crucial when I later began to set up City Gateway.

I grew up in a privileged home in Dumfrieshire in southwest Scotland, and came to London in 1990 to train as a professional singer at the Royal Academy of Music. During my time there I became a Christian, which made an enormous difference to my life. I started to reappraise what was important, and found myself thinking much more about other people. As a result, but contrary to most people's advice, I gave up my professional pursuits for a year and stood for election as the student union president. I won the election, and became very involved in representing those people who I thought were getting a rough deal.

Afterwards, I decided to pursue a political career rather than a musical one. To my great surprise, I was accepted on a scheme run by Christian Action Research and Education (CARE) to be a researcher for a very inspiring Member of Parliament called Andrew Rowe. At the same time I helped to run an organisation called Christians in Student Politics, which was designed to support those people who were encouraging Christian values in their universities.

The CARE scheme lasted for a year, and it was afterwards that I couldn't find a job. Eventually, I did find a job I enjoyed with the European Youth Forum to lobby on issues of long-term unemployment. I was able to examine ways of getting people back into jobs, which I was extremely fired up about, having just been unemployed myself. Later, I was employed as a lobbyist with an organisation called Christian Solidarity Worldwide, and it was during this time that I decided to found City Gateway.

I had felt challenged to do something practical about my faith for a number of years. Henri Nouwen once wrote, 'You are a Christian only so long as you constantly pose questions to the society you live in. . . So long as you stay unsatisfied with the status quo and keep saying that a new world is yet to come.' I remember when I was still a music student talking to someone whom I respected enormously for her Christian leadership, who suddenly announced that she had given up on her faith. I asked her why and she said that within the Christian community she didn't see any evidence of people living out authentic, biblical faith. I was intrigued by this, given that I considered myself to be living out my faith. She challenged me from the Bible to see that Jesus called us to reach those who God identified as requiring special help, such as the poor, the outcast and the homeless. She argued that we were failing to do that, and therefore the authentic gospel was not being lived out.

I was deeply challenged by this, and so together with a couple of friends we decided to look at Scripture, pray and reflect on it. It struck us that one of the problems was that we simply weren't coming across such people because of the places where we lived and worked. We realised that, if our friend was right, we needed to change our lifestyles and live in surroundings where we could be among those less privileged than ourselves. At around the same time I had been very challenged by a missionary called Jackie Pullinger, who works with drug addicts in the poorest parts of Hong Kong. I listened to her speaking on tape. There was a particular phrase she used at Oxford University when she responded to some students who asked if they could go to help her in Hong Kong. She turned round and said to them, 'But what about the housing estates here?' And I thought, 'What about the housing estates here? I don't think I have ever been on one. I don't even know any.' So I began to pray and think of how I could get to live on a housing estate in London.

I applied for council housing, but found out that I wasn't eligible. I wondered how on earth I was ever going to get to live in one of these places. But about this time, a friend of mine, who was also praying in the same way, came across an advert for a house to rent in Spitalfields in East London, and explained that he believed this was where we should go. A group of us went to look at it. We discovered that it was situated right in the middle of a housing estate and so we decided to move there. Within a year-and-a-half a group of 15 people from a church called St James the Less in Pimlico also moved to the area, and joined our local church, called Christchurch, in order to help impact the community.

Spitalfields is a ward within Tower Hamlets, which is only 500 yards away from the City of London. It is an area of some of the highest density housing in Europe. It is not untypical for six people to live in two rooms, and I have heard of cases where up to 14 people live in such conditions. Statistics show that 83 per cent of the population are Bengali, and shockingly the infant mortality rate among their community is higher than in Bangladesh. About 40 per cent of the Bengali community are unemployed. Spitalfields also has a dreadful problem with drugs – a local survey revealed that the cheapest heroine in London is sold in Brick Lane, which is the street where I live. But perhaps most soberingly of all, the average age of those buying drugs in the area is just 14.

Although we had moved to the area and were living in the middle of the estate, it was still very difficult to build contacts with people. Some were so high on drugs that it was impossible to communicate with them. I began to get very frustrated, and wondered how we could ever reach these people. We prayed and thought about it, and had the idea of starting some kind of IT training and employment scheme for young people who were long-term unemployed.

A friend of mine and I wanted confirmation for this idea and so both took an afternoon off work to pray about it. Three things happened that evening. As my friend left, he happened upon a community office where he went in and talked through the idea to see what they thought. They said that it was a fantastic idea, that they had been hoping that someone would develop such an initiative, and that there was a lot of government funding available (it didn't work out quite so easily in the end!). Second, I went off to meet a friend who hadn't seen me for a while and told him about the plan. He told me he had been best man to someone who developed a similar project in Seattle, which had now grown into a multi-million dollar company. And third, another friend phoned up and said she had been praying and felt that she needed to do something in IT for long-term unemployed people in East London and did I have any ideas? All this was out of the blue and happened on the same night! We decided to take it as a green light and we were very excited. I presumed that the whole thing would be up and running within three months.

The three of us prayed and worked hard to find the funding to get started. Two of us stopped working five days a week and went down to two. We wrote enormous papers and went to see everybody under the sun. We applied for all sorts of funding and kept believing that the Lord was going to lead us into this great funding pot. I remember working into the early hours of the morning night after night. There were so many opportunities which we thought were going to provide the big breakthrough. However, time after time, at the last minute, after putting in so much hard work, our applications were turned down. Although there were numerous pools of funding, no one was prepared to get behind us because we didn't have a track record.

This went on for 16 months, and after a while we couldn't bear it any more. We had prayed our socks off and we couldn't understand what was going on. Some people were saying that we just had to have more faith. Others said that God clearly wasn't in what we were doing because he hadn't delivered. Eventually, even close friends decided they could not carry on supporting this without seeing real results. That led to a terrible sense of pain and loss for me. I can truly say that those 16 months were the hardest times I've ever been through. The knowledge that one has to persevere in the face of opposition is an exhausting one, especially when you are getting advice to the contrary and colleagues are leaving because they are beginning to believe that the vision is wrong. It was a very lonely and tiring time. There was the sense in which I had given up my career for this and now I didn't know what the future held. It became an issue of pride to see whether or not I could make the thing happen. But in the end I got to the point where I said to God, 'OK, cards on the table, this is it. I have to die to this completely because the idea of starting the project has become my raison d'être. That is unhealthy, and anyway I can't do it.'

However, I still felt God wanted City Gateway to happen. I remember praying, 'I believe this idea is from you, regardless of how far I might have got the details wrong, and I am willing for you to do anything in order to bring it to fruition. If you want me to give this to someone else then that is what I will do.' I began to feel that the Lord was asking me to go through a process of changing the constitution of the project. I realised that I should think about setting the project up as a charity instead of a company of which I was the owner, so that I made myself fully accountable and transparent to a group of trustees. I was so tired and exhausted that I had no energy to fight with God over such a change and so began making the necessary arrangements. Interestingly enough, it was almost as soon as that happened that we received our first offers of funding and we were finally able to begin to get City Gateway off the ground. That was in September 1999.

The vision of City Gateway is simple: to break through the glass wall that divides Tower Hamlets from the City of London. Living in Spitalfields enabled me to see that on the west side of Brick Lane there is great affluence and prosperity, but on the east side there is tremendous poverty and a lack of training and opportunity. Such a close juxtaposition means that those living in Tower Hamlets are very aware of the sense of injustice. City Gateway's goal is to create a dual carriageway through this glass wall, by allowing the unemployed of the Bengali community access into the City and at the same time enabling a way for the City to get involved with Spitalfields.

Our aim is to equip the long-term unemployed with the skills and opportunities they need to enter the market place. In order to do this, our first move was to develop a foundation course in IT skills. It runs for twelve weeks, and we teach all the basic software packages such as Word, Excel, Powerpoint and Access for those who have little or no IT experience. The course leads to a Microsoft Office Users Professional Examination which is taken on line and in which we boast an 80 per cent pass rate. Afterwards we arrange for each student to have four weeks in a placement, which is a key component in developing their practical experience of the work place.

More recently, we have developed our own web design course, which once again teaches all the main software packages and gives the students the opportunity to design web sites for charities. We are also thinking about launching a course to train CISCO technicians, because there is a big market for people to work in setting up computer networks.

We recruit students through a variety of means. We get people in the church out onto the streets to knock on people's doors and offer the course by word of mouth. We also go down to the Job Centre to chat to unemployed people, and the staff there are very good at referring people on to us. On top of that we advertise in the local newspaper. Our target group is young adults aged 18 to 25, but we aim to get a mix of age and experience so that those who are more motivated help to foster an environment that encourages the rest. We are now on our fifth course and have trained over 70 people to date. Everybody who comes to us is unemployed prior to starting the course, but having completed it 70 per cent enter into and remain in full-time work. Some of these also go on to further education, which itself is an amazing change from their previous situation.

The barriers to professional employment are huge. Entering a nine-to-five working culture is a massive cultural leap for someone from three generations of unemployment, who is used to living off the dole and various other benefits. It requires a huge amount of education, much of which needs to address issues that we often take for granted. The environment we grow up in, as well as the example of our parents, instils in most of us a positive subliminal preparation for work. But for a whole generation of Bengali people this is often not the case. Some grow up in homes where English is not spoken and where there is no space to work or study, because they have to share their

bedrooms and even their beds with their parents and sib-
lings. We have also found that many of those we work
with find it difficult to understand why they have to be at
work on time every day, since their parents, who have a
very different sort of time culture, have never brought
them up to be anywhere on time. Another problem we find
is that students often don't think twice about having a day
off whenever they feel like it – they presume it is accept-
able to simply not turn up. These things are not because
they are inherently lazy, but because they have not been
brought up in the psyche of the Western working ethic. But
the practical upshot of it all is that it is realistically very
difficult for these young people to aspire to the working
opportunities that are out there.

I remember one very personable Bengali 19-year-old,
who successfully completed the IT foundation course and
came to do work experience for two days a week in my
work place with me. After a couple of weeks he simply
dropped out and left without telling me. It was very
frustrating because the office had timetabled some admin-
istrative tasks for him to do. I kept phoning and leaving
messages on the answerphone to find out what was going
on, but I heard nothing for three weeks. Eventually he
came in and had lunch with me, and explained that his
father had bought a bigger house for the family and was
insistent that he gave up his work experience to earn some
money to help meet the bills. It was very frustrating
because his obligation to provide for his father in the short
term prevented him from tapping into the new opportunities that would have brought far greater benefits to both
him and his family in the long run.

Our aim is to break down these barriers to professional employment, and one of the key ways we have attempted to do that is through the development of our mentoring system. In effect, our mentors act as surrogate parents. For example, they phone up on the first day of a new job to say, 'You are going to work today. Are you up? Have you got a shirt ironed? Have you got your shoes polished? Make sure you are polite to your manager. Make sure you get there on time,' and so on. There are no hard and fast rules, but usually they will meet the student they are mentoring face to face for roughly one hour a week as well as talk on the telephone. An important part of each mentoring relationship is that our mentors put aside one lunchtime in their diary every couple of weeks when the student with whom they are working can come into their office to talk about how things are developing. It is a big deal for a student to be bought lunch, to have to dress up for the occasion and have to get there on time to talk through their career and potential dreams and visions. It all works very well. Our mentors also undertake to pray regularly for their students, because we are convinced that prayer is a vital key to ending the degenerative condition of long-term unemployment.

Our office is designed to simulate a working environment so that our students get used to working in a corporate setting. In fact, we now go as far as to actually do some of our training in the offices of City firms. So, for example, we do a day session in Price Waterhouse Coopers and another in Lewis Silkin solicitors. We even spend a training day in the House of Commons. It is all part of breaking through the glass wall.

We also incorporate employment training as part of the course material. For three hours a week we address issues of letter and CV writing, interviewing, time management, appropriate dress and language, and general office culture. Sometimes we get people from the City to come and teach on these skills. We also do team-building exercises to explore students' gifts and to build their confidence. As part of the course we also run a development training weekend, for which we usually take the students to Wales. Some of them have never really seen the countryside before, and I remember one person who had never even been to west London. We take them on activities such as pot-holing, climbing and swimming in the sea. It is a great opportunity to build the relationships which are at the core of our work. We have bonfires on the beach and chat late into the night. We also put on special nights back in London, such as meals and film nights, which are once again aimed at continually building strong relationships.

We look at the needs of individuals in a holistic manner, which means we are open to addressing their physical problems (for example if they are struggling with drugs), their emotional needs (problems at home, etc.) as well as their spiritual needs. City Gateway is an expression of our love of Christ, and so is by its very nature evangelistic. We believe that the message of Jesus Christ is good news and therefore are up front with our students right from the start of the course about the basis of the faith that inspires us to do this work. At the beginning of the course, we will say to the students, 'You may be interested in why we run City Gateway. Well, this guy in the Koran you know as the prophet Isa, we know as Jesus. We reckon he came to help us to love our neighbour. That's what City Gateway is all about.'

However, we never force Christianity on people, and we would never want to. It would be wrong and unbiblical for us to require our students to read Christian literature or make any kind of affirmation of the Christian faith. The reality is that if we did we would have no credibility in the community. We would be seen to be culturally imposing. No one is forced into doing anything Christian on the course, and people are welcome to just come for the IT training and leave the Christian bit out altogether if they choose to.

However, in practice we find that people normally want to know what the Bible has to say on the numerous topics that come up. For example, once a week as part of the foundation course, we have an 'Issues Session' where the students bring to the table any subject they want to talk about. It can be anything from marriage to drugs, sex, credit card fraud, or under-age driving. It provides the opportunity to talk about values and the issues that prevent people from getting on in life. In this context it is often appropriate for us to share our own values. We will also offer to pray with people if they would like us to.

For example, there is a young man who comes from a very difficult background. We first came into contact with his family when his younger brother made a petrol bomb out of a milk bottle and threw it at us outside my house. We were excited when his elder brother decided to come on our course. He was mentored by one of our trustees, did well, and passed the exam.

We had great hopes for him as he was a very sociable

young man. But three months after finishing his work experience, he came to see us in a terrible state. His father had left the family and his brother's behavioural difficulties had got worse. His mother was disabled, and because he felt financially responsible to look after her, he had got involved with a bad crowd who were engaged in crime. He'd got hooked on heroine, had been caught in a shop involved in credit card fraud and had ended up in a police cell for four days in Scotland. He came to us because he had nobody else to turn to. Our staff offered as much practical help as they could, but they said ultimately the only person who could really help him was Jesus Christ. They offered to pray for him, which he said he would like. He got off heroine and was actually treated pretty leniently by the court. His mentor helped him to get his CV back together, so that he could find a new job. It is this kind of story which is what we are all about.

City Gateway is linked with Christchurch in Spitalfields, where I am the worship leader. The majority of the mentors come from the church, as do a good many of the trustees. Although the church does not support us financially, they pray for us regularly and we have the chance to give them regular feedback. We now employ four members of staff, and I have been able to return to full-time work as a parliamentary lobbyist. I still oversee the project and go to the team prayer meeting once a week. I am also the chair of the trustees and act as a mentor on each course we run.

Our initial funding came from Tearfund, who gave us £10,000, and the Mercers Company, who gave us £4,000. Tearfund have been particularly supportive. Not only were they willing to back us on the basis of our faith when we had no track record, but they have since kept in contact to find out how we are doing and to offer ongoing prayer support. Now that we have a track record, other funding is easier to find. We have secured grants from the European Social Fund and the Single Regeneration Budget (which we have to match with private funding). Deutsche Bank has also recently agreed to fund one of our salaries and other individuals give very generously. Our budget this year is nearly £90,000.

As we look towards the future, our vision is to continue to see the Kingdom of God come in the Spitalfields area. This may mean that in time City Gateway becomes more than just an IT training base. We have thought about the possibility of a family centre or a drug rehabilitation unit, as well as various other options, which would allow us to respond at greater depth to the community's issues. What I know from my experience so far is that none of this will ever be easy. I believe that things that are worthwhile entail sacrifice. However, without doubt, the difficulties help to keep us dependent upon God. The principle I have learned is to praise God for our sufferings, because they produce perseverance, and perseverance produces character, which produces hope and a hope that never disappoints. Ultimately, I believe that the cost is worth it.

I think of one other student from the project. When he left school at the age of 18 he saw that there were two career paths that were successful in his community. He had a choice between joining the police and trading in drugs. He wanted to do what was right, and so he applied to the police for a job. Unfortunately, he was rejected on the grounds that he was not fit enough – so instead he eventually started trading in drugs. Two years later, we persuaded him to come to City Gateway for some IT training. He absolutely loved the residential weekend away. He was on a total high, because he climbed cliffs, saw the sea and even some sheep – all for the first time in his life! On the way home he told us that City Gateway had given him the opportunity he needed to get out of the drugs trade. I will always remember him saying, 'I am going to make it to the top because City Gateway has given me hope for the first time in my life.' Today he works as an estate agent, and his words still echo in my mind, because as long as City Gateway keeps giving people hope for the first time, then it is worth all the sacrifice in the world.

Relevant contacts

The Basic Skills Agency provides information, research and ideas for training people in basic skills. See: www.basic-skills.co.uk

Community Logistics is a professional consultancy service working with community groups to help them realise their aims, especially in the areas of IT and recycling projects.
1 Bower Terrace
Tonbridge Road
Maidstone
Kent ME16 8RY
www.commlog.org

Interwork provides retraining, help for the unemployed, mentoring and consultation.
Swallowdale
The Quarry
Tisbury
Salisbury SP3 6HR
Tel: 01747 870 670

Pecan is a highly successful re-training project, celebrated by national government, which offers churches and individuals practical advice on setting up social action projects. Their 'Project Hatching Workbook' costs £10.00.
1–3 Atwell Road
London SE15 4TW
Tel: 020 7740 9200
Email: welcome@pecan.org.uk
www.pecan.org.uk

The Vines Centre Trust is an unemployment/retraining and furniture recycling project which can offer advice and general consultancy.
Vineswood House
Gas House Road
Rochester ME1 1PN
Tel: 01634 406 245
Email: paul.robinson@vinescentre.org.uk
www.vinescentre.org.uk

Further Information

Faithworks provides a network and range of resources, including books, tours and a consultancy service to equip churches to serve their neighbours, and to work with politicians to renew communities. The 'Faithworks Directory' provides a comprehensive guide to the organisations and resources that can assist local projects.

Nathan Oley

The Oasis Centre

115 Southwark Bridge Road

London SE1 0AX

Tel: 020 7450 9050

Email: faithworks@oasistrust.org

www.faithworkscampaign.org

Useful Contacts

In addition to the contacts listed at the end of each chapter, these organisations can provide a general service to churches that wish to enhance their community work. This list provides a tiny selection of agencies that have a track record of advising churches on how to set up and maintain a wide range of successful community projects.

Act International (New Frontiers International) provides a series of practical booklets and a network of expertise which can enhance a range of church-based social projects.
Ms Penny Relph
81 Poverest Road
Orpington
Kent BR5 2DZ
Email: pjprods@dircon.co.uk
www.n-f-i.org

154   FAITHWORKS 2: STORIES OF HOPE

Anthony Collins Legal Advisers provide specialist legal advice to churches.
Mr John Iles
St Philip's Gate
Waterloo Street
Birmingham B2 5PG
Tel: 0121 212 7400
Email: john.iles@ascollins-col.co.uk

British Association of City Missions has considerable expertise in communicating and demonstrating Christian care through a wide range of projects in the inner city.
Birmingham City Mission
75 Watery Lane
Middleway
Birmingham B9 4HN
Tel: 0121 766 6603
Email: mission@globalnet.co.uk

Christian Action Networks equip churches across Britain to work together in order to engage in community development.
Julia Collingbourne
The Evangelical Alliance
Whitefield House
186 Kennington Park Road
London SE11 4BT
Tel: 020 7207 2123
Email: cans@eauk.org
www.eauk.org

Churches Child Protection Advisory Service provides advice on the essential safeguards which are necessary to ensure that children are safe in churches.
PO Box 133
Swanley BR8 7UQ
Tel: 0845 120 45 52
Email: info@ccpas.co.uk
www.pcca.co.uk

Community Action Network is a practical mutual learning and support network for social entrepreneurs setting up community based projects.
The CAN Centre
Mezzanine Floor
Elizabeth House
39 York Road
London SE1 7NQ
Tel: 020 7401 5310
Email: canhq@can-online.org.uk
www.can-online.org.uk

Community Action Safety and Training provides training courses, consultancy, strategic planning and networking.
Jaz Greer
4 Merridale Road
Littleover
Derby DE23 7OJ
Tel: 01332 763 263
Email: office@cast-derby.org.uk
www.cast-derby.org.uk

Community Matters (National Federation for Community Organisations) publishes books and pamphlets on various aspects of managing small volunteer-led organisations.
8–9 Upper Street
London N1 0PQ
Tel: 020 7226 0189
www.communitymatters.org.uk

Inland Revenue – Charities
Meldrum House
15 Drumsheugh Gardens
Edinburgh EH3 7UL
Tel: 0131 777 4000
www.inlandrevenue.gov.uk

National Association of Councils for Voluntary Service will help you find your local council for voluntary service.
3rd Floor Arundel Court
188 Arundel Street,
Sheffield S1 2NU
Tel: 0114 278 6636
Email: nacvs@nacvs.org.uk
www.nacvs.org.uk

National Children's Bureau provides information, advice and support for those working with young children in both statutory and voluntary services.
8 Wakley Square
London EC1V 7QE
Tel: 020 7843 6303
Email: amckerrell@ncb.org.uk
www.ncb.org.uk

National Council for Voluntary Organisations and the National Council for Volunteering. The main representative body for the voluntary sector in England. Provides advice, information, training and publications on all aspects of running a voluntary organisation.

Regent's Wharf
8 All Saints Street
London N1 9RL
Tel: 020 7713 6161
Email: ncvo@ncvo-vol.org.uk
www.ncvo-vol.org.uk

Pecan is a highly successful re-training project, celebrated by national government, which offers churches/individuals practical advice on setting up social action projects. Their 'Project Hatching Workbook' costs £10.00.

1–3 Atwell Road
London SE15 4TW
Tel: 020 7740 9200
Email: welcome@pecan.org.uk
www.pecan.org.uk

Rebuild is a coalition of 60 organisations working together to encourage and equip churches to run 'Community Weeks'.

Alicia Meijer
c/o 16 Kingston Road
London SW19 1JZ
Tel: 0870 3300 212
Email: info@rebuild.org.uk
www.rebuild.org.uk

SEED trains and equips churches for social action, especially in the areas of homelessness, youth crime, unemployment and drug and alcohol dependency.

Vickers House
Priestly Road
Basingstoke
Hampshire RG24 9RA
Tel: 01256 363 447
Email: peter.hawkins@bigfoot.com

The Shaftesbury Society produces a guide to community research and has developed an 'Action for Change' network which offers support, training and materials for church-based projects.

Church Development Services
16 Kingston Road
London SW19 1JZ
Tel: 020 8239 5555
Email: info@shaftesburysoc.org.uk
www.shaftesburysoc.org.uk

Social Workers Christian Fellowship provides advice and expertise for those who work with children and young people, especially regarding child protection and mental health issues.

54 Manchester Road
Manchester M27 5ET
Tel: 0161 950 7312
Email: mhall@btinternet.com

Tearfund offers a 'Church, Community and Change' consultancy and six-month process for churches who wish to get more involved in meeting the needs of their communities but don't know where to start.

100 Church Road

Teddington

Middlesex TW11 8QE

Tel: 020 8977 9144

Email: enquiry@tearfund.org

www.tearfund.org

Faithworks

Actions Speak Louder Than Words

by Steve Chalke

Our political leaders are beginning to talk about the real need for greater involvement by voluntary groups – including churches, Christian charities and other faith-based agencies – in providing welfare care. The Faithworks Campaign is committed to make sure that all the encouraging rhetoric we've been hearing from Westminster translates into reality.

This informative, provocative book will help clarify the issues and equip us to respond both to human need and to those in government that influence welfare issues and funding.

'Rumours about the church's untimely death have been rumbling around influential places for a long time. The Faithworks Campaign is an exciting opportunity to put such rumours to rest.'

– JOEL EDWARDS, General Director, Evangelical Alliance

'The Faithworks Campaign – a message and movement that needs to be heard.'
– DAVID COFFEY
General Secretary, the Baptist Union

'The Faithworks Campaign is a challenge and an encouragement to local Christians to be intimately involved in their local communities.'
– JAMES JONES, the Bishop of Liverpool

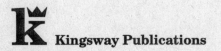 **Kingsway Publications**